Published by
AMERICAN MALACOLOGISTS, INC.
P. O. Box 2255
Melbourne, Florida USA 32901

Originally published as a French edition:
**Coquillages des Côtes Atlantiques
et de la Manche** by Les Éditions du Pacifique, 1979
Translated from the French by B. E. Picton

Library of Congress Catalog Card Number 78-74491
ISBN 0-915826-05-4

Printed in Japan

ph. bouchet
f. danrigal
c. huyghens

sea shells
of western europe

american malacologists

contents

introduction

From the Dover Straits to the Spanish border the French coasts of the Atlantic and the English Channel have a coast-line measuring some 3,020 km (1880 miles) which includes as diverse habitats as the forests, alpine pastures, peat-bogs or heathlands of the continents. In the sea these habitats are the estuaries, *Zostera* (eelgrass) beds, boulder fields, underwater caverns, surf-beaches, saltmarshes, etc. There are thousands of different animals which live in these various situations.

The interest which we show in our native fauna today is not a recent development. Our knowledge of the shells of the Atlantic coasts and the English Channel has been accumulated by generations of naturalists, biologists and enlightened amateurs, who, since the beginning of the 19th Century have felt the urge to explore the natural history of the sea. The names of Montagu, Forbes, Hanley, Alder, Michaud and above all Jeffreys should be mentioned. By 1869 Jeffreys, in his ``British Conchology'' had described and figured virtually all of the species of the British Isles and the English Channel. After him Marshall, Chaster, P. Fischer, H. Fischer and Dautzenberg brought to our knowledge the very small species which had escaped the previous workers, or those

Opposite: The North Atlantic Drift (Gulf-Stream) warms the waters of Europe: Plymouth is at the same latitude as New-foundland! The isotherms correspond to the surface temperatures in summer.

4

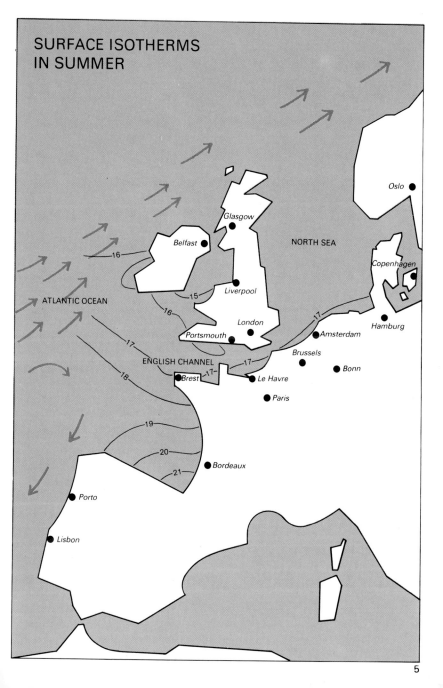

SURFACE ISOTHERMS IN SUMMER

of the Bay of Biscay and in particular the Basque coast, which had been little explored until then.

At the same time the development of marine laboratories allowed zoologists to study the biology and ecology of living animals on the spot. The most important laboratories on the Channel and Bay of Biscay coasts are those of Plymouth (Marine Biological Association of the U.K.), Roscoff (C.N.R.S.) and Arcachon (Faculté des Sciences de Bordeaux). We have been helped by these laboratories, and also those of Dinard (Laboratoire du Muséum National d'Histoire Naturelle) and Biarritz (Musée de la mer) in the production of this handbook.

In the Mollusc group, (Phylum Mollusca), which is characterised by the presence of a foot, the species are grouped into a number of major categories called classes.

Bivalves (top left) and Gastropods (bottom right) live in all situations, while the Scaphopods (bottom left) are animals of sand or mud and the Polyplacophores (top right) are only found on hard substrates.

The Molluscs are divided into seven classes.

The **Bivalves** as their name indicates have a shell consisting of two valves joined by a hinge: about 200 species on our coasts.

The **Polyplacophores,** or chitons, whose shell is made of eight jointed plates: about 15 species on our coasts.

The **Scaphopods** or tusk shells, have a shell like an elephant's tusk: 6 or 7 species on our coasts.

The **Gastropods:** by far the most numerous, walk on their foot. Their mouth is armed with a toothed tongue, the radula. The shell is spiral in the *Prosobranchs* (c. 350 species) and reduced or absent in the *Opisthobranchs* (c. 200 species).

The **Aplacophores,** wormlike creatures without a shell (a dozen species in our area); the **Monoplacophores** which are found in the abyss and the **Cephalopods** should also be mentioned.

A given species of mollusc does not live just anywhere; like a bird or a mammal each species has certain biological or ecological requirements which restrict it to a particular habitat: seaweeds, rocks, estuaries, beaches, etc. Superimposed on this horizontal separation is a vertical distribution, particularly important in our tidal seas. The tidal range is 14 metres in the Bay of Mont St. Michel, one of the greatest ranges in the world, it is only 8 metres in the region of Brest and 5 or 6 metres in the Bay of Biscay.

These factors of habitat and position on the shore, to which we must add seasonal variations, explain why our temperate coasts are able to support so many species of animal. With a total of nearly 800 species this part of the European coast is one of the best known in the world; it is thought that about 99.5 % of the species present are known. This handbook clearly does not aim to help find the 0.5 % which remain, but to familiarise people with some of the most attractive of these molluscs in their living state.

fauna of the seaweeds and zostera beds

Seaweeds provide shelter for the marine animals of the intertidal region, protecting them from heat and desiccation, and also providing food for the numerous herbivorous molluscs which exploit them. Whether it be a limpet or a winkle each species has its own ecological preferences which determine its position in the intertidal region, from the supralittoral or splash zone to the kelp *(Laminaria)* zone.

It is only in the most exposed sites or where the rock is very soft or friable that the plant cover is missing. The algae, like all other plants with chlorophyll need sunlight for growth; it is the red algae which are, in general, the least exacting and can therefore survive in the deepest water. The limits of algal growth are about 20 metres in an estuary with murky water but 50 to 60 metres in an area of clear water and as deep as 100 metres in parts of the Mediterranean. Not all of the many species of seaweed, red, green or brown, are of the same ecological importance; many are very small and provide little of interest to marine animals, either as food or as shelter; others, on the contrary, because of their large size and the density of their populations form algal forests sheltering a variety of herbivorous molluscs which are more or less strictly associated with them.

Opposite: The Laminaria *zone, only uncovered at the lowest spring tides, is the richest zone accessible to the shore-collector. One* Laminaria *plant provides a mosaic of microhabitats for other species, each inhabited by characteristic animals: the holdfast, the stipe and the frond.*

the splash zone

In the supra-littoral region there is often a fine black turf which covers the rocks, just below the lichens. This black turf, looking like a lichen, is called *Lichina pygmaea,* and shelters in its humid cover numerous insect larvae, small crustaceans and two tiny molluscs, a gastropod called *Littorina neritoides* and a bivalve, *Lasaea rubra.* Each measures only a few millimetres when fully grown, and both have developed novel methods of reproduction in this harsh environment, moistened only every 15 days at the spring tides of the full and new moon.

in the rock pools

Certain red algae incorporate lime into their tissues and become very stony and hard. These calcareous algae look like thin pink incrustations or little pink bushes, and line the high level rock pools which are occupied only by animals which can survive heating by the sun and dilution by rainwater. Here we find sea anemones, a few small crustaceans and two or three molluscs: the limpets, of course, but also a couple of top-shells, *Gibbula umbilicalis* and *Monodonta lineata.* We also find these species in this region on the apparently bare rock, amongst the barnacles. Their radulae, especially that of the limpet, are very hard and mineralised, in order to scrape the microscopic film of algae from the surface of the rocks.

how the limpets return home

While during low water the animal is found in a pool, when the tide is in, the limpet leaves its place to feed and returns to exactly the same spot several hours later. Each individual has in fact a regular home where the contours of the shell fit exactly to the uneven rock surface. This, together with the force of adherence of the foot, in the order of 3 to 4 kg per square centimetre, explains why it is difficult to dislodge a limpet without the benefit of surprise.

Another common species which is found at the high levels alongside the limpets is a winkle, the rough winkle, *Littorina saxatilis*, the object of considerable research on the part of ecologists for the past 20 years. At birth the young winkles measure only a few millimetres and grow up close to their mother. There is therefore very little cross-breeding between populations and this explains the uniqueness of each population.

in the middle of the wrack

Descending now with the tide we come to the belt of wracks which are so characteristic of the coasts of Cornwall or Brittany. The wracks are the first example which comes to mind when we talk of the formations or forests of algae. They consist of the large brown seaweeds of the genus *Fucus* and continue as far down the shore as the beginning of the large *Laminarias* of the infra-littoral fringe, which only uncover at the lowest spring tides. Here there is a mass of vegetable material, capable of feeding lots of herbivorous browsers, but which is in fact little exploited by molluscs, presumably because of its tough leathery consistency.

At the higher levels we have seen two species of winkle, a third species *Littorina obtusata* is one of the molluscs which scrapes these large seaweeds for its food.

the *laminaria* zone

Just below the intertidal region the kelps are the home and food of the blue-rayed limpet, *Patina pellucida*, a primitive gastropod in which the limpet-like shell is decorated with blue lines. The blue-rayed limpets scrape and remove the surface of the seaweed and the film of diatoms which covers it, and at the same time hollow out a home for themselves in the stipe or holdfast of the kelp.

In the winter and early spring egg masses in the shape of a lens, 5 to 8 mm across can be found amongst the brown and red algae of the *Laminaria* zone. These are the eggs of *Lacuna pallidula* another herbivorous species closely related to the winkles.

the sea hares

The sea hare is one of the gastropods in which the shell is reduced to a small horny plate incapable of containing the animal. Four species of sea hare are found on our coasts, but are very difficult to tell apart. They browse on seaweeds, preferring red algae, but they are not very fussy and will also eat green algae and small brown algae.

the seaweed piercers

The green seaweed *Codium tomentosum* gets its specific name from its large cells, which give the plant a velvety appearance. *Codium* is found on rocks in rock-pools in the intertidal area, or even on rocks which are left dry at low tide. Its large cells are used in a very interesting way by two species of opisthobranchs, *Elysia viridis* and *Placida dendritica,* which pierce the cell walls with their radula-teeth, which are modified like an awl: the molluscs suck out the cell contents of *Codium* including the chloroplasts, which contain chlorophyll and colour the animals green.

the ormer

Lots of other gastropods which are more or less herbivorous live in the lowest region of the shore; more or less herbivorous because besides a main diet of algae they also eat organic detritus and small fragments of rock. A typical example is the ormer, *Haliotis tuberculata,* catches of which are carefully regulated on the north coast of Brittany to prevent depletion of the stocks: experiments have been started to grow the ormer by aquaculture.

The topshells like *Calliostoma zizyphinum* (Painted topshell), *Gibbula cineraria* (Grey topshell) and *Gibbula pennanti* live together in these boulder fields covered with seaweeds. The sexes are separate but they do not copulate; the female releases her eggs into the water where they are fertilised by spermatozoa discharged by the males in their vicinity.

the beds of *Zostera,*
the marine flowering plants

The fauna of the *Zostera* (eelgrass) beds can be grouped in a similar fashion to that of the seaweeds. *Zostera* looks rather like a grass and is in fact a flowering plant, which has returned to the sea. These beds contribute a biological habitat of special characteristics entirely due to the eelgrass.

the *Zostera* disease

The present state of these beds can only be understood in the light of the great epidemic which from 1931 to 1933 decimated the *Zostera* on all the European coasts. Starting on the Atlantic coast of the U.S.A. at the beginning of the summer of 1931 the disease, caused by a bacteria, a microscopic fungus or a virus, no one is sure which, reached the English Channel and the Atlantic coasts of France in 1932 and as far as Denmark in 1933. This disease caused the disappearance of the beds of *Zostera marina* resulting in modification of the substrate and disappearance of all the associated flora and fauna. Here is what Prenant said at the time about the Bay of Quiberon: "In all the places in this region except one, *Zostera marina* has disappeared or retreated considerably. The species only survives in small scattered spots. These important changes in the flora have not been without serious repercussions for the fauna. Indeed these repercussions have also been very damaging for the fishermen of the Morbihan region, who deplore them." Seventeen years later, in 1949, Wilson recorded that at Salcombe, near

Plymouth, the disappearance of the *Zostera* had caused a sinking of the beach by two feet (60 cm).

The recovery of the *Zostera* beds has been very slow and today they cover a far smaller area than they did before 1930. This disease, coupled with more and more stupid human intervention, explains the impoverishment shown by the beds in the last 50 years.

...and at the same time

At the present time a new menace threatens the *Zostera* beds, following the accidental introduction of *Sargassum* to the English coast. Fortunately a rapid mobilisation of algologists and a campaign of eradication of the *Sargassum* plants has meant that only a small population in the region of Portsmouth has become established. The danger lies in the fact that the *Sargassum* would be able to take over the habitat of the *Zostera,* without providing the same ecological environment for the associated fauna, with a consequent imbalance.

A horde of small gastropods are found on *Zostera* leaves, which they scrape with their radulae: for instance *Lacuna vincta,* whose spawn is blue-green when it is laid, becoming white or yellowish as the embryos develop; *Cantharidus striatus,* which lays its eggs on the leaves in April, also a number of small species of Rissoids which are for the most part only 6 or 7 millimetres in length. *Bittium reticulatum* shows a preference for the leaves, whereas *Bittium simplex* prefers to live in the tangle of small algae, sponges and sea-squirts which cover the ground amongst the bases of the *Zostera* plants. It is also in this virgin mini-forest that we find the nudibranch *Aegires punctilucens,* and the bivalve *Modiolus adriaticus* which anchors itself by its byssus threads to the base of the stems, and filters the water for its food.

the dustmen of the sea

One species is often noticed because of its eggs which

are small, flattened, transparent capsules fixed in a row of 3 to 15 along the length of the *Zostera* leaves. These are the eggs of the netted dog-whelk, *Nassarius reticulatus,* the adult of which spends most of its time hidden in the sediment searching for its food. In actual fact the netted dog-whelk is not only found in the *Zostera* beds, but also on bottoms of coarse sand and fine gravel. The role of the dog-whelk is to clean the *Zostera* bed of dead and dying animals, which it tastes or smells through its long siphon; it plays the role of the vulture in tropical regions.

threatened species

It is perhaps interesting to conclude by discussing a small nudibranch *Corambe testudinaria* which was originally described at the end of the last century, living on the leaves of *Zostera* in the bassin d'Arcachon. This species occurred in *Zostera* beds from Arcachon to the north coast of France and apparently was very common. It has now become extremely rare, probably as a result of the disease of 1932, and very few individuals have been found in the last 20 years. A comparable example is that of *Rissoa membranacea,* formerly common from the Mediterranean to the coasts of Scandinavia. It is still abundant in the south, less common in Brittany and has become rare or very rare further north in the British Isles and Denmark.

From the black *Lichina* of the high levels to the *Codium* of the pools and the *Zostera* beds the marine plants offer lots of habitats, each of which is exploited by a unique fauna. It is clear that, even if no species is conspicuous because of its large size, very few places are left vacant in this ecological assemblage. It is also very worrying to record that the displacement of a single element in this assemblage results in a series of imbalances and may take a very long time before the damage is repaired, especially faced with a shore more and more subject to the action of man.

boulder beaches and rocky overhangs

Everyone has at some time turned over the rocks at low tide to search for crabs, sea urchins or starfish. Much rarer are those who have seen, alongside these little monsters, the more obscure, camouflaged animals which exist in this habitat in a diversity which makes the seaweeds and *Zostera* beds a virtual desert by comparison. At its best the underside of the boulder is entirely covered with sponges, sea-anemones, sea-squirts, bryozoans, hydroids and barnacles, which find both support and shelter from the light and from predators in this position. In general the underside of a boulder is richest when it is uncovered least by the low tide, and when it is least embedded in sand at its base. A similar fauna is found when diving on fallen rocks.

one year to live and die

The small species which are found here are nearly always annuals, that is to say, their life-cycle (birth, growth, reproduction and death) is completed in one year or less. According to the seasons the fauna can vary considerably beneath the same piece of rock; one species, which is common in August or September, will be absent in the spring, and in the same way another species will never be found in the winter. Therefore the naturalist or the diver is able to visit a landscape which changes considerably according to the time of year.

Opposite: Boulder beach on the south coast of Brittany. This spot was previously very rich in molluscs and crustaceans, but is devastated every summer by fishing; even young animals and mature females are taken.

the molluscs without shells

The most striking element of this fauna is certainly the abundance and colouration of the nudibranchs; more than a hundred species of these shell-less molluscs live on our coasts. Their bright colours are often cryptic in their natural surroundings and without a minute examination it is very difficult to spot the bright red dorid amongst a mass of red sponge, or another species which hides itself, out in the open one might say, on flat colonies of bryozoans. The study of nudibranchs can only be carried out on living animals as they lose all of their colouring and much of their shape when they are preserved. The pioneers like Joshua Alder and Albany Hancock knew this when in 1855 they described most of the species occurring on the British coasts, with magnificent coloured illustrations. No doubt this explains why there still remain undescribed species on the coasts of the English Channel and the Bay of Biscay. The coasts of Brittany and the Basque coast are particularly rich, and still insufficiently explored.

sponge-eaters

What are these unknown species? Let us look first at those which are associated with sponges. ``The sponges of the French coasts?'' some may ask. The well known bath sponge is in fact only one amongst many species; more than 250 species live in the English Channel and the continental shelf of the Bay of Biscay.

The most common predator of these sponges is the sea lemon, *Archidoris tuberculata,* which grows up to 12 cm (5 in). In winter and spring it is found under boulders where its scrapes off the sponges with its radula. In contrast with the shelled gastropods (whelks, winkles and topshells), the sea lemon is a hermaphrodite.

the nudibranchs of the basque coast

At least 20 other dorids feed, like the sea lemon, on

sponges. The most beautiful of these are found on the Basque coast, for instance *Hypselodoris valenciennesi,* blue with yellow lines, or *Chromodoris purpurea,* white and lilac in colour. These very colourful nudibranchs belong to a tropical family which reaches its northern limits of distribution in the Bay of Biscay. Very little is known of their biology. *Berthella,* a close relative of the nudibranchs, feeds only at night. It swallows enormous pieces of sponge, which it then takes several days to digest.

The dorids are not the only molluscs feeding on sponges, there are also the needle whelks, *Triforis,* which have the distinction of a sinistral shell, that is a shell coiled in the opposite direction to most other gastropods. Its proboscis, small enough to enter the osculae of the sponge and reach the softer internal tissues, *Triforis* completely avoids the outer parts of the sponge, which are densely packed with silica spicules. The keyhole limpet, *Diodora apertura,* is found beneath rocks where it scrapes away at the sponges; its shell resembles a limpet, but has a hole at the top through which the anus of the animal empties.

searching for food in calcareous boxes

Other nudibranchs feed on bryozoans, little colonial animals which take the form of spreading crusts or little erect trees. Bryozoans are a whole animal group which most people have never even heard of, probably because none of them is either edible or venomous or commercially of any importance. Oyster-growers know them well, however, as one species attaches itself to their limed tiles at the same time as the oyster spat, and competes with the growth of the young recently metamorphosed oysters. They commonly call this bryozoan "crêpe". *Schizoporella linearis* is also a sort of "crêpe" which forms the exclusive food of the dorid *Onchidoris depressa.* The method used by this mollusc to find the living matter in the middle of the boxes, bulkheads and calcareous spines of the bryozoan is a great mystery.

The magnificent *Antiopella cristata* browses on an erect bryozoan, *Bugula,* which grows under rocks or rocky overhangs. Each of the processes which covers its back contains a part of its digestive gland, which is divided into hundreds of branches.

You are bound to ask what the little soft sacks are which send out a jet of water when they are pressed. These are also a sort of animal, the sea-squirts or ascidians, certain sorts of which are eaten in the Mediterranean. In the Atlantic and the Channel none is eaten by man, but many are eaten by molluscs.

the cowrie which lays its eggs on its food

The cowries, *Trivia* spp., are great eaters of sea-squirts. Their shells are rather like the tropical cowries, whose lustre is due to the mantle of the animal which normally covers it and secretes a sort of varnish. These small cowries are well known to French children who call them ``grains de café'' or ``cochon rose''.

They feed on several species of sea-squirt but prefer to lay their eggs in a hollow dug into a colonial sea-squirt. *Lamellaria perspicua* lays its eggs in exactly the same way on other sea-squirts. It is a prosobranch, but looks like a nudibranch; its delicate internal shell is entirely enclosed by the mantle, giving the impression of having no shell. *Lamellarias* prefer the Didemnid ascidians, which they mimic perfectly.

a competitor of the cowrie

Another common feeder on the sea-squirt *Dendrodoa,* which can be found in clusters beneath rocky overhangs, is the white dorid *Goniodoris nodosa*. This is its exclusive food, and it is very common on both coasts of the English Channel. Further south its prey disappears and it becomes very rare in the Morbihan region and completely absent south of the Loire. *Goniodoris* needs cold water for its reproduction.

what attacks a poisonous prey?

Sea-anemones have very few enemies in nature. Their tentacles contain stinging cells which inject with the aid of a harpoon a deadly poison. This is used to capture their food (small fish, crustaceans and molluscs) and also to defend them from attack. The Aeolid nudibvanchs, however, are specialised in the impossible task of feeding on sea-anemones. How is this achieved? The Aeolid approaches the anemone very gently stretching out its sensory tentacles and secreting copious amounts of mucus. This mucus prevents the poisonous harpoons from penetrating and holding the sea-slug, and the anemone is eaten piece by piece.

Seven species of nudibranchs which eat sea-anemones occur on our coasts. The best known and largest is *Aeolidia papillosa,* which can reach 10 cm (4 in) long. Like the *Goniodoris* it prefers cold water for its reproduction and reaches its southern limits in our region. Its characteristic spawn is common beneath rocks in the spring. The *Aeolidiella* are found throughout the region but the *Berghia* are only found in the south.

a small crustacean which spends its whole life inside a sea-slug

Even though they are very cunning animals, the Aeolids are attacked by other animals even more cunning. It is not unusual, on the Basque coast or in the Bassin d'Arcachon, to see amongst the greenish-brown cerata of *Spurilla neapolitana* two little violet sacs. These are the eggs of a small parasitic crustacean, which is completely hidden in the body of the nudibranch and reveals only its egg-sacs to the outside. Only the larvae are mobile; the adult copepod, completely deformed by its parasitism, is incapable of movement. Other Aeolids eat hydroids. A hydroid is a little colony of animals each of which is like a miniature sea-anemone. Each animal measures between a half and five millimetres and the colony is usually between one and fifteen centimetres in height. About forty species of Aeolids are predators on hydroids in our region. Some of these eat the individual polyps while others eat the whole colony at once. There is no point in describing these here; in the photographic section we show some of the commonest or most beautiful species.

scallops and saddle-oysters

The rocks are also the shelter and support of several bivalves, such as the scallops *Chlamys varia* and *Chlamys distorta*, which attach themselves to the rock with byssus threads, just like the mussels. If the conditions should become unsuitable the animal is able to cast off this mooring and reattach itself in a spot which it prefers.

The saddle-oysters in contrast are totally incapable of moving; their byssus is very large and calcified, and passes through a hole in the lower valve of the shell. The animal is literally cemented to the rock. Even when it dies and the fragile mother of pearl valves fall away on to the beach, the byssus remains on the rock as a little calcareous concretion.

We saw earlier how the netted dog-whelk played the role of dustman in the *Zostera* beds and on sandy bottoms. Beneath the rocks this role is taken up by a smaller species, the thick-lipped dog-whelk, *Nassarius incrassatus*.

Also living beneath these rocks are the sting winkles, *Ocenebra*, which bore into the shells of bivalves or barnacles with the help of an acid secretion. When the hole is big enough they eat the oyster without opening it. *Ocenebra erinacea*, called the boring whelk by oyster growers, is a real pest on the oyster beds.

TERMINOLOGY OF THE INTER-TIDAL ZONES AS CHARACTERISED BY THE BELTS OF BROWN ALGAE

balcis and the sea-cucumbers

In previous sections we have seen molluscs as the victims of various parasites, usually worms or crustaceans. In contrast some molluscs are themselves parasites, for example, the whole family of eulimids feeds at the expense of echinoderms, holothurians (sea-cucumbers), starfish and sea-urchins. *Balcis crosseana* for instance penetrates the skin of a holothurian with its proboscis and sucks up the internal fluids. Another family of small gastropods which are temporary parasites, is the *Pyramidellidae*. They are occasionally found in all sorts of habitats, and there are over 50 species which are often very difficult to identify. We do not intend to discuss this group any further as their biology is still very little known.

living inside the mountains.

After the rock support and the rock shelter we now come on to the rock fortress; the piddocks are capable of boring into some of the hardest rocks to make themselves a refuge. The work of drilling is entirely mechanical, and is carried out by the sharp ridges which decorate the valves. The piddocks are found commonly in limestone, mudstones, or in the encrustations of calcareous algae, but they avoid the very hard metamorphic rocks, though it is possible to find them in Gneiss.

take care to replace the rocks

As we have shown, the rocky shore is an extremely complex habitat in which a multitude of species interact in relationships of predation, parasitism or competition. However this equilibrium is an extremely fragile one, depending entirely on the orientation and position of the boulder. Turn a rock over and leave it upside down and the upperside with the seaweeds on it is deprived of sunlight and water movement. In a few days the algae are dead and rotting, killing at the same time all their associated fauna. Conversely the underside of the rock is exposed to the drying action of the wind and sun, which is very rapid. In a few hours 80 % of the attached animals will be dead. Obviously the other species, which rely on the fixed organisms for food, will soon be dead as well.

After a couple of days a boulder which is left upside down and not returned to its place is completely devoid of life, all of its previous richness is gone. It will take many months for a new equilibrium to be achieved on this rock, for the algae to grow on the upper side and for the light-sensitive animals to recolonise the underneath.

The conservation of our shores can only be achieved by the understanding of the people who visit them. These beautiful, rich and varied boulder shores will only be preserved if the fishermen and naturalists are vigilant, and always apply this golden rule: never leave any boulder upside down; replace them exactly where they were.

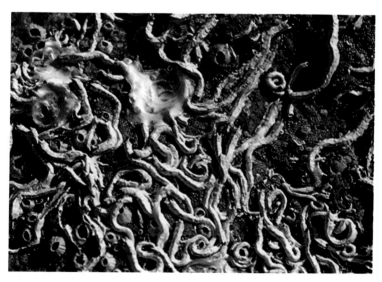

All life has been killed on this boulder left upside-down by a fisherman. The animals living in the shelter of the rocks are unable to stand the bright light, and above all, the heat of the sun, and are all dead within a few hours.

estuaries

the life of estuaries

Neither river nor sea, the estuary is a unique place where land meets sea and fresh water meets salt. The physical characteristics of this system (brackish water and heavy mud deposition) provide a unique and original habitat to which a few molluscs have become well adapted. Let us look at an estuary for one tidal cycle, for instance, the estuary of the Tamar, the Somme or the Escaut. It is clear that a large part of the banks is not covered by neap tides: this is the saltmarsh, well represented at Mont St. Michel. At low tide the exposed surface is much greater, with vast exposed areas of mud, the mudflats. These two zones are found in all the estuaries of Western Europe. They each support a specialised flora and fauna, and as biological habitats they are both rich and poor, rich in individuals but poor in the number of species.

the animals of the saltmarsh

With succulent plants and plants with hard dry leaves side by side the saltmarsh is the site of an interesting meeting of pulmonates and prosobranchs, that is to say snails breathing with a lung and those breathing with gills. This illustrates at once the amphibious character of this habitat. These gastropods are all very small, growing up to only 7 or 8 millimetres. They live at the base of the plants on the humid soil, or beneath wood deposited by the high tide, or under stones. The pulmonates are

Opposite: An English Channel estuary at low tide, showing the mudflats and the saltmarsh. The muddy expanses are the site of great biological activity, but unfortunately many councils see them as ugly areas and turn them into dumping grounds, refuse tips or areas for industrial development.

represented by *Phytia myosotis* and *Alexia bidentata*. *Pseudomelampus exiguus* is a species which is only found on the Basque coast, and elsewhere in Madeira. The prosobranchs are represented mostly by the genus *Assiminea* which is adapted to live in estuarine saltmarshes. *Assiminea grayana* occurs in the Channel and the North Sea, *A. eliae* at Arcachon and on the Basque coast. Another species, *Assiminea ostiorum,* was described from the Bassin d'Arcachon and was only known from this locality. Despite considerable searching it has never been rediscovered. Has it disappeared? The saltmarsh is a particularly vulnerable habitat and the development of ''reclaimed'' land has resulted in the disappearance of hundreds of acres of saltmarsh in the last 20 years.

in the mud

The great expanses of mud which are exposed at low tide are the favourite haunt of large numbers of wading birds which come down to feed. Their victims are a few crustaceans, some worms, but mostly bivalves. One of these, is *Cardium lamarcki,* a close relative of the edible cockle, but only found in brackish water. It survives equally well in the reduced salinity of estuaries and in the high salinity of the saltmarsh channels (Guérande, Ile de Ré). The peppery furrow-shell *Scrobicularia plana* lives in the same habitat and its presence is indicated by a small star-shaped depression made by the siphons through which the animal feeds. The gapers *Mya arenaria* and *Mya truncatula* are found buried much deeper in the mud. They were the objects of considerable trade in the last century, both for human consumption and for fishing-bait, and as a result have a plethora of local names, ''patagau'' in La Rochelle, ''old maid'' in Southampton, ''cockle-brillion'' in Northern Ireland and ''smirslin'' in the Shetlands. The colourful names have now all disappeared to leave only "sand-gaper" or "clanque" in their place.

0.3 cm² per individual

One gastropod which does not fear overpopulation is *Hydrobia ulvae,* whose density may reach 32,000 per square metre. Its normal size is 6 to 7 mm but some individuals reach 10 mm. These large individuals are nearly always parasitised by the cercaria larvae of flatworms, which live in the gonads or digestive gland of *Hydrobia.* Fish or birds which eat these infected snails also become infected, and the larvae develop into adults in their digestive tracts. The life cycle of this flatworm therefore needs two hosts: *Hydrobia,* which is prevented from reproducing by parasitic castration, and a fish (or bird) in whose digestive tract the adult flatworm lives. In the faeces of the fish are flatworm eggs which can reinfect the gastropod after they have been released into the sea. Thus both hosts are indispensable to the life of this parasite.

A couple of other gastropods live in the green mat of *Vaucheria* which covers the mud in places. These are the ascoglossans *Alderia* and *Limapontia,* which pierce the cells of *Vaucheria* and suck out the contents in the same way as *Elysia.*

the importance of protecting estuaries

The relatively monotonous fauna of the estuarine habitat makes it far less attractive than the rocky shore or the *Zostera* beds, but it has a very high productivity and is important to the large numbers of birds and fish which feed on the mudflats. Unfortunately these areas are often chosen for the establishment of industries, which add their characteristic pollution to that already carried by the river. Clearly there is very little natural habitat left today in the estuaries of the Thames, the Seine or the Adour, and the way things are going it is difficult to say what will be left of these habitats in 10 or 20 years time.

sandy beaches

Carpet-shells, cockles and razor-shells are some of the large number of edible shellfish which live in sand or gravel. Perhaps you have raked at low tide to feed yourself, then you can imagine the amount of sand which must be worked to extract the 5000 tons of the warty venus or the 1000 tons of carpet-shells which are collected commercially every year.

the great variety of bivalves

As in the Sahara where the animals hide in the soil by day and only come out at night, the life in a sandy beach is entirely buried and only shows itself when the tide is in. The carpet-shells (palourdes) *Tapes decussatus* and the golden and pullet carpet-shells (false palourdes or pissoues) *T. aureus* and *T. pullustra* remain closed when the tide is out, waiting for the arrival of the waves to extend their siphons to feed and breathe. It is true to say that all the bivalves of the sand have much in common. They all feed and respire by filtering the water and nearly all reproduce by releasing their eggs free into the water where fertilisation occurs. We do not find the elaborate variety of life styles of the gastropods in the bivalves. This is not to say, however, that all bivalves are the same; one species for example may filter plankton of only 3 to 5 microns in diameter, while another may filter particles of 10 to 20 microns. Some species live in coarse gravelly sand

Opposite: A sandy beach at low tide. The bivalves and worms, which are the main inhabitants of these ever-moving expanses, have strict requirements as to the particle size of the sand, as this determines the degree of aeration and water circulation between the grains. Some bivalves filter the organic particles suspended in the water while others take particles deposited on the sediment surface.

while others are only found in fine sand.

It is the coarser sands with a good amount of shelly material which are the richest. Large numbers of venus clams, carpet-shells, trough-shells *(Spisula solida),* cockles *(Cardium edule, C. tuberculatum, C. crassum),* tellins, hatchet-shells and razor-shells are found in these sediments. During the harsh winter of 1962/63 the warty venus *(Venus verrucosa),* which is particularly sensitive to cold, was very badly hit, and these beds have taken a long time to recover. It is only in the last 3 or 4 years that the situation has returned to normal. All of these species are used as food, at least among the local people.

the necklace-shells - borers of bivalves

Living out of sight does not necessarily mean living safely for a bivalve. They live in even greater terror of the necklace-shells than of the starfish. Necklace-shells are gastropods which burrow in the sand to catch them. Once it has found a bivalve the necklace-shell encloses it in its muscular foot and starts to drill into the shell. This process is rather different to the drilling in the sting winkle or dog-whelk however; the necklace-shell uses an enzyme to dissolve the organic matrix of the shell, and then breaks up the calcareous crystals with its radula. The end result is always the same: a neat round hole with bevelled edges through which the necklace-shell devours the unfortunate bivalve. There are two common species of necklace-shell on our shore: the large one, *Natica catena* eats trough-shells or small venus clams, while the small one, *Natica alderi,* eats tellins or hatchet-shells. When they are spawning, the necklace-shells mix their eggs into a collar-shaped cake with sand and mucus, hence the name necklace-shell. The spawn-collar of *Natica catena* is slightly less than one turn and that of *N. alderi* two or three turns. *Philine aperta* is yet another predator on bivalves. It moves through the sand like a streamlined bulldozer and grinds up small bivalves, foraminifera and small gastropods with its hard gizzard plates.

A few other gastropods also live in these sands: the auger-shells, *Turritella,* are buried like bivalves and are also filter feeders. The wentletraps, for instance, *Clathrus clathrus,* have a mysterious way of life. It is known that many tropical and Mediterranean wentletraps feed by sucking the body fluids of sea-anemones, so it seems likely that our species feed in the same way, but this awaits confirmation.

Dentalium, the scaphopod mollusc, which is shaped like an elephant's tusk, also lives in sand. It feeds by collecting organic detritus with its minute tentacles, and also eats small foraminifera. The eggs of *Dentalium* are often used by biologists to study embryological development, and these results allow general conclusions to be drawn about the embryology of many other invertebrates.

the surf beaches

The wide exposed beaches, like those of Aquitaine, Vendée or Bas Poitou, and also some beaches in the English Channel, are very barren. In this realm of breaking waves the sand is constantly stirred up and only the wedge-shells and trough-shells can survive. The commonest of the wedge-shells is *Donax vittatus* which is eaten locally and known by the name of ''Pignon''. The wedge-shells burrow when the tide falls and come to the surface when it comes in again, so that they are carried about by the waves.

the winkle

The gravelly and pebbly shores do not really make up a separate habitat. Bivalves which can tolerate coarse sediments, such as the carpet-shells, are found here with a few species which have no precise habitat requirements, such as the winkles and whelks, which also live on the oyster-beds and amongst the *Zostera*. The edible winkle *(Littorina littorea)* is a littorinid like the other winkles we have encountered amongst the seaweeds. It feeds on the organic detritus in the fine muddy deposits which cover the ground between the pebbles. Because of this behaviour winkles are deliberately grown in the oyster-beds to help keep them clean. A large proportion of the winkles eaten in France are imported from Ireland.

an avid carrion-eater

The whelk, sometimes known as ''bulot'' in the markets of large French towns, is one of our largest gastropods. It can be over 12 cm (5 in) long. Like the dog-whelks, the whelks, *Buccinum undatum,* can smell at a considerable distance the dead bodies or dying animals which they eat. When they are egg-laying, the females gather in small groups to produce a collective egg-mass. The eggs are enclosed in packets of 6 to 10 in a white fibrous bubble. These egg sacs are then stuck one on top of the other on to a stone or a large empty shell. Sometimes they can be found broken off and cast up on the beach after a storm. These white spongy masses may be over 20 cm (8 in) across. All the embryonic and larval development of the whelk is completed inside the case made by the mother, and, when the young hatch, after several weeks, they are fully-formed miniature whelks.

living between the sand-grains

The large bivalves are the most obvious inhabitants of this sandy universe, and it is only in the last 30 years that a vast variety of life has been discovered living between the sand-grains. Tiny animals, never more than 3 or 4 millimetres in length, spend their whole life in this situation, living on a sand grain. The little *Caecum* is the commonest mollusc, with as many as several hundred living in one litre of sand. Their remarkable adaptation to this life in sand must be very ancient as species of *Caecum* are found in sand all over the world. At the end of the last century, de Folin, captain of the port of Bayonne, specialised in their study, and was sent sand samples by correspondents all over the world.

A hundred years later the study of interstitial fauna is more popular than ever, and even in Europe, where many zoologists are dedicated to this study, much is still unknown. It must be remembered that one or two metres below the sand the seawater is in contact with the water table. Under a ton of sand is a characteristic community of tiny worms, crustaceans and molluscs.

rarities under rocks on the sand

It is interesting to mention another strange small community of small animals which live under large rocks partly buried in the sand. In the chapter on the animals of rocky shores we saw the species which live abundantly under the rocks: encrustations of sponges, sea-squirts, hydroids etc. In contrast sandy shore rocks have none of this animal cover: they are completely bare. All the more surprising then to find here gastropods *(Tornus subcarinatus, Alvania lactea),* a bivalve *(Pseudopythina setosa)* and a chiton, all of which have the reputation of being very rare. In fact this is because their peculiar habitat is largely unknown. What do they eat, and how do they reproduce? Absolutely nothing is known about these species, and the same is true of the subterranean brackish-water species which we briefly considered in the last chapter.

To say that all the estuaries of the Channel, the North Sea and the Bay of Biscay are the same is not far from the truth. Exaggerating to only the same degree we could say that no two sands are the same. A variety of habitats and fauna exists which surprises us for a situation which we believe in advance to be extremely uniform.

oyster- and mussel-farming

the decline
of the natural beds

It is difficult to imagine today the immense beds of native oysters (*Ostrea edulis*) which existed on all the coasts of Europe at the end of the 18th and beginning of the 19th centuries. At that time there was practically one continuous bed from Denmark to Spain. Excessive collection due to the markets created by the industrial revolution and over-enthusiastic use of the dredge wrought havoc in these beds in the middle of the last century. The establishment of the railways permitted exportation of the oysters to the large towns where the growing populations consumed vast numbers of oysters. In Billingsgate, the London fishmarket, 500 million oysters were sold in 1864 alone.

Both reproductive adults and young were collected and nowhere was left unexploited. By the end of the century the enormous natural banks of oysters were no more than a memory. In 1887 Heape wrote in reference to the banks in the Plymouth region: "There were many beds here, now not a single one remains. The decline of the Cattewater banks can certainly be attributed to overexploitation by dredging, but it seems to me more likely that the general decline is due to dispersion of kaolin residues from the china clay industry, which has polluted the beds." Joubin reports similar results in France: "The old fishermen still talk of the rich oyster beds which used to be found throughout the bay of St. Brieuc. They have now completely disappeared or been reduced to insignificant vestiges. It is too late to try to control this now. The Bay

Opposite: At the end of June in the "river" at La Trinité (Morbihan region). The limed tiles are ready to be immersed to collect the spat of the native oyster. South Britany has 3500 hectares of oyster beds and 40 million tiles for spat collection.

of St. Brieuc has been depopulated not only of the shellfish but also of all other animals worth fishing for."

When the oysters had practically disappeared from all the French coast, protective legislation was rather belatedly established and vigorously enforced. By 1905 for example, at Tréguier on the north coast, dredging was only allowed on one day of the year, and then only for 45 minutes. On this day the whole fishing fleet would assemble, waiting for the signal, a cannon shot, to start fishing. Another shot 45 minutes later and fishing was finished for the year. Nowadays the laws are just as severe where they are applied to natural beds in deep water.

the government authorises
start of oyster culture

Meanwhile, in 1883, H. Coste was instructed by the French Ministry of Agriculture to study the possibility of growing oysters. It was this man who became the founder father of oyster farming. Following a voyage to study the situation in Italy and around the French coasts, he developed the idea of using spat fixed on collectors to establish artificial oyster-beds.

the life cycle of the oyster

When they are reproducing the oysters take on a milky appearance, then the white liquid which gives them this appearance becomes grey. This happens during the months without an "R" and in mid-summer the oysters are fully mature.

Originally made of bundles of wood the collectors are now limed tiles which are immersed at low tide level a little while before the predicted date of spat settlement. After initial growth of the spat (about 8 months), the oysters are detached for growth in the beds until they are 2 or 3 years old. They are then sent to be fattened and cleaned before being dispatched for sale and eating.

accidental introduction...

At about this time American oysters were being imported on the English coast to make up for the failure of the natural beds. Unfortunately other less desirable species were also imported with these oysters. In 1887 the first shells of *Crepidula fornicata,* a slipper limpet from the coasts of Labrador and Florida, were found on the Lincolnshire coast. By 1895 the coasts of Essex were largely overrun, the coasts of the Netherlands by 1922, and the Belgian coast by 1930. Today the American slipper limpet has colonised suitable habitats on all the west European coasts from the North Sea to the Iberian peninsula.

...and deliberate introduction

This slipper limpet is not the only species to come to us from America. The Quahog or Clam arrived in Britain in about 1860, probably via the kitchens of the passenger liners plying between Europe and the United States.

In this case it was a species with economic potential and so it was deliberately introduced into several rivers in Dorset and Essex where thriving populations still exist today. In France the Clam was introduced in about 1910 in the mouth of the Seudre and most recently into ''river'' of Bono (Morbihan region). Colonies of this species in the Netherlands and in the port of Ostend also deserve mention.

All of these regrettable accidental introductions should have been treated with greater caution as they introduce new and unpredictable elements into the habitats of our native species.

Unfortunately this is not always the case, especially where commercial interests are involved, though the vigilance displayed by the French Fisheries Institute and the importers of the Japanese oysters *Crassostrea gigas* should be commended. In Japan there is a flatworm which often feeds on oysters. The introduction of this worm could prove disastrous for our oysters so after leaving Japan the oysters must undergo a freshwater treatment which kills the flatworms without harming the oysters. This is the sort of care which should always be taken.

the portuguese oyster

So far we have been discussing the native oyster, which was the primary oyster for commercial production up to 1920. Between 1860 and 1868, following the over-exploitation of the beds in the Arcachon region, the local fishermen were unable to satisfy the demands of their customers. They therefore decided to import Portuguese oysters, which prospered in the mouth of the Tagus. Between 1869 and 1875 they planted between 25 and 30 million Portuguese oysters per year in the Bassin d'Arcachon. In 1868 the ship ``Le Morlaisien'' encountered a severe gale on her return from Lisbon, and was unable to enter the passage into Arcachon and took refuge instead in Gironde. Meanwhile the oysters began to rot and had to be dumped into the sea between Saint Christoly and the Verdon. These oysters found very favourable conditions at this spot and soon formed extensive semi-natural beds of extraordinary richness.

As early as 1890 the Poole Oyster Company was importing Portuguese oysters to the English coast and by 1914 they were being either grown or stored at numerous points on the French channel coast; Fécamp, Dives, Courseulles, Saint Vaast. However neither there nor on the Atlantic coasts of Brittany have any natural beds appeared.

The culture of the Portuguese oyster has replaced the native oyster in the Bassin d'Arcachon and in Charente-Maritime. On the south coasts of Brittany both species are grown. The region of Marennes is well known for its green oysters due to the presence of a microscopic planktonic alga (*Navicula ostrearia*) which is eaten by the oyster as it filters the water. This region, with its 3,800 hectares of 29,000 beds, is the most important oyster-growing region in Europe, with an annual production of 40,000 tons, being 60 % of the French national production.

diseases of the oyster

In the course of the last 10 years the Portuguese oyster has gone from one disease to another, the most recent being the ``gill disease'', which killed 40 % of the oysters on some beds. During this period there have been massive importations of foreign spat, principally from Japan.

mussel-farming—as early as the middle ages

The first mussel farms were reputedly established in the 13th century by an Irishman, Patrick Walton, who was shipwrecked in 1235 at the Point of Escale, near the port of Esnandes (Charente-Maritime). To him is attributed the invention of the stakes on which the mussels grow and the special flat-bottomed boats which slide over the mud and allow people to tend the farms. The Bay of Aiguillon (Vendée) was the place where this industry was first established.

Oyster-farming is, in comparison, a very recent human activity, with nothing like the history of mussel-farming. It should first be explained that there are two species of commercial mussel in Europe. The edible mussel, *Mytilus edulis,* extends from the White Sea to as far as the Mediterranean, and the Mediterranean mussel *Mytilus galloprovincialis,* which is larger (for example the large mussels in Spanish paella) and extends as far north as Cornwall, where it is known as the Padstow mussel.

In France the mussel-farms (stakes, flat-beds and rope culture) are established under licence from the Fisheries

Department (Affaires maritimes) which grants a concession for 25 years. These concessions can only be granted in areas where the water is known to be clean. The water must satisfy the standards of the scale of bacteriological water quality as defined by the Scientific and Technical Institute of Marine Fisheries. In France there are about 15,000 of these concessions partially or entirely exploited for the growth of mussels, with an annual production of 40,000 tons. The consignments dispatched for consumption are packed, as in the case of the oysters, with a cleanliness label bearing the number of the establishment which is distributing them (called a certificate of cleanliness) and the date of dispatch.

the enemies of mussels

Like the oysters, mussels have many natural enemies: starfish, which force the valves half open and eat the mussel inside; seagulls and oyster-catchers which break open the shells with their beaks while the tide is out. The mussels are also the prey of the dog-whelk, *Nucella lapillus* which secretes an acid to bore through their calcareous shells. The gastropod then consumes the bivalve (through this hole) in an operation which takes 6 to 12 hours altogether.

Occasionally you may eat a mussel which crunches between your teeth, but not because it is full of sand or badly washed. This is because of a small crab, the pea crab, which lives in the gill cavity of the mussel sheltered from the outside world. It is not a parasite, but feeds on the waste products of the mussel, and is therefore called a commensal. Another crustacean *Mytilicola intestinalis* is a small parasite which lives in the intestine of mussels, and results in their emaciation and eventual death.

Opposite: Farming of mussels, in plastic pockets in the Bay of Veys (Normandy). In the last 10 years shellfish farming has been started in many bays on the Normandy coast.

the sub-littoral region

The sea bed covers a far larger area than that of the narrow intertidal strip which uncovers twice a day. In this book we are limiting ourselves to the species of the continental shelf, which may be seen in the markets or by sailing on a day trip on a small trawler.

the maerl

The continental shelf is always illuminated in its shallower parts, permitting algal growth. The red encrusting algae, which grow in little calcareous bushes, are particularly common, and are called maerl. This maerl is very abundant in the Bay of Lannion, and in the region of Glénans. Here it has been exploited, or rather overexploited, for a long time as lime for agricultural use. The maerl extends throughout the infra-littoral region and is uncovered in some places by the lowest spring tides. Its fauna is very rich: fish, crustaceans, worms and molluscs all hide among its branches. *Tricolia pullus,* a small gastropod with a thick calcareous operculum, lives in this situation feeding on diatoms and algal debris. *Cantharidus exasperatus* has a similar way of life. The most characteristic element of this fauna is a species of chiton, *Callochiton laevis* whose eight shell plates are marked with red, pink and white, providing excellent camouflage amongst the maerl.

living with
the dublin bay prawns

The trawling grounds for Dublin Bay prawns or scampi are the great muddy plains of the Bay of Biscay. This is also the habitat of *Aporrhais pespelecani,* the well known pelicans-foot shell, and of *Armina,* a flattened nudibranch which feeds on sea-pens.

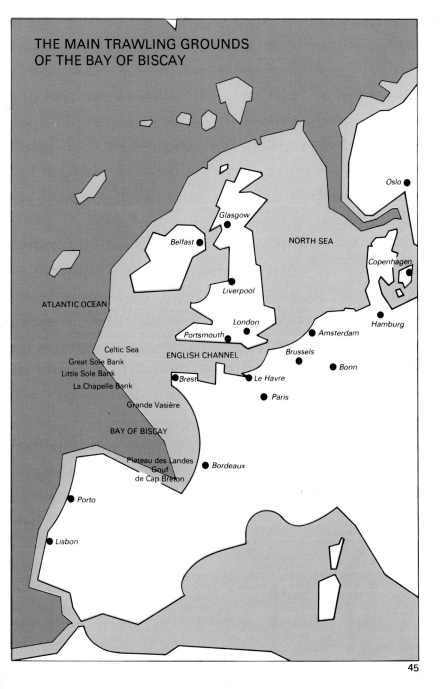

THE MAIN TRAWLING GROUNDS
OF THE BAY OF BISCAY

Oslo

Glasgow

NORTH SEA

Belfast

Copenhagen

Liverpool

ATLANTIC OCEAN

Hamburg

London

Portsmouth   Amsterdam

Celtic Sea   ENGLISH CHANNEL

Great Sole Bank   Brussels

Little Sole Bank   Bonn

La Chapelle Bank   Brest   Le Havre

Grande Vasière   Paris

BAY OF BISCAY

Plateau des Landes   Bordeaux
Gouf
de Cap Breton

Porto

Lisbon

45

the great scallop

The great scallop (*Pecten maximus*) lives in beds on sand and muddy gravel bottoms in the infra- and circa-littoral zones. With an annual production of 20,600 tons, the fishery for great scallops is an important source of revenue on the Brittany coast. In spite of severe restrictions these beds are finding it difficult to support the pressure of fishing and it seems possible that we will see the development of aquaculture for this species in the next few years. The great scallops' natural enemies are starfish. It can "smell" these at a distance through the sensory tentacles around the edge of its mantle and then escape by swimming off, clapping its two valves together like a set of false teeth.

On these same grounds lives a real brute of an opisthobranch, *Scaphander,* whose gizzard plates work like a grindstone crushing bivalves, tusk-shells and foraminifera for its food.

on the spine
of a sea urchin

Montacuta substriata is a tiny bivalve only 3 to 4 mm across, but is very easy to find. It lives associated with the large burrowing sea-urchins *Spatangus*, which are sometimes taken in the trawls. The spines on the underside of the urchin must be examined very closely to see the *Montacuta*, attached by a fine byssus thread. The bivalve cannot live without the sea-urchin, but does not cause it any harm; this is another example of commensalism, which has nothing to do with parasitism.

the strange life
of *philbertia* the hunter

The turrids are small gastropods, ranging from one to a few centimetres long, which live on soft ground from the continental shelf to the abyss. They belong to the same evolutionary line as the tropical cone-shells, and like them feed by hunting with a poisoned harpoon. This harpoon is in fact a modified radula tooth, which is hollow and filled with poison from a poison-gland. When the prey, usually a worm, is discovered the *Philbertia* injects it with venom to immobilise it and then swallows it whole.

This use of venom is very different to its use by octopuses and cuttlefish, which first catch their prey, fish, crustacean or other mollusc, using the suckers which cover their arms. When the jaws (beak) bite into the flesh of the fish, only then are the venom glands able to come into operation as they have no injection device.

The cephalopods are the most highly evolved molluscs by a long way. The study of their behaviour has become a subject in itself and entire books have been written on the subject. We have no intention to add to this literature here, but can thoroughly recommend ``Kingdom of the Octopus'' by Frank W. Lane (Jarrolds, London).

eight arms, five hundred suckers

Octopuses live in small underwater caves or make a home under a large rock. These are generally easy to spot because of the food refuse, of crab carapaces and empty shells which litter the ground outside the entrance. In the octopuses the sexes are separate but there is no mating in the normal sense of the word. The male and female remain about one metre apart and one of the eight arms of the male is transformed into a hectocotylus. A hectocotylus is a specialised arm which detaches from the male and carries the spermatozoa into the branchial cavity of the female. The female then lays her eggs in strings at the entrance of her cave; one female may lay as many as 150,000 eggs. The female broods her eggs, not by sitting on them as birds do, but by circulating the water around them. She also remains near the eggs until they hatch and keeps away any predators.

The octopus has eight arms and no shell; the cuttlefish and squids have ten arms and an internal shell, which is the cuttlebone and the pen of the squid. Squid often live in groups and have complex communal mating behaviour, which has been popularised in the films of Jacques Cousteau.

The cuttlefish and squid suffer due to the appetite of the Japanese, as most of the 9,500 tons caught annually on our coasts, mainly on the sands of Olonne and Cherbourg, are exported to Japan.

the queen of camouflage

During the winter the cuttlefish migrate to the deeper waters of the open sea, but return to the shallow coastal waters to breed in the spring. Their eggs are well known, as the black sea-raisins which can be found attached in groups of 6 to 30 on *Zostera* plants and seaweed. The cuttlefish's skin contains vast numbers of pigmented cells which are able to expand or contract instantly, changing the colour of the animal to correspond with its background. This superb camouflage combined with their speed of movement, makes the cephalopods practically invulnerable. They also have the ability to disguise their flight by discharging a cloud of black ink, emitted at the same instant as a change of colour from dark to light. This makes it easy to see why few fish are as efficient hunters as the cephalopods.

Without doubt, a night spent on a small trawler would produce many other species. Much deeper at 300 to 350 metres, the continental slope begins. It is a steep drop, indented with submarine canyons and with a rich and varied fauna, but only accessible to oceanographic vessels with special equipment.

Opposite: The presence of octopuses is normal in the Bay of Biscay, but in the Channel they have never really re-established themselves since the severe winter of 1962/1963.

the species

51

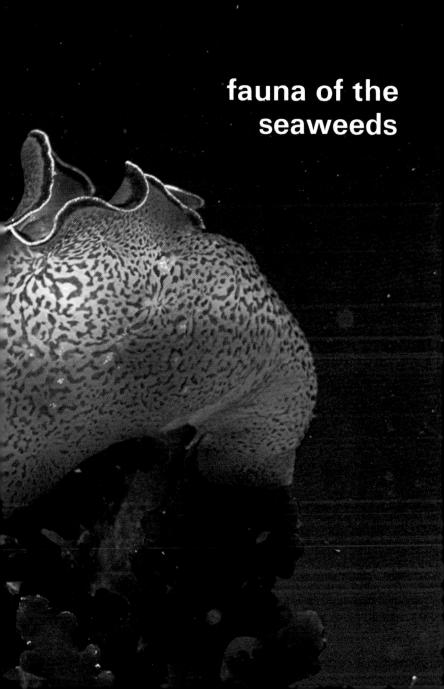

**fauna of the
seaweeds**

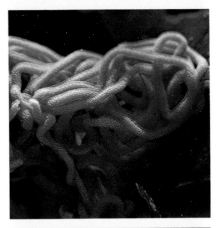

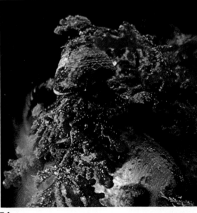

Previous page: a young sea-hare Aplysia punctata *(40 mm) browsing on red seaweed. The morsels of seaweed are held by the vice-like jaws and are literally shredded by the radula-teeth and accessory spines. Adult sea-hares can be very large, some monsters are 30 cm (1 foot) long and weigh 1.5 kg (3 lb). Sea-hares are hermaphrodite that is both male and female at the same time. Copulation occurs in chains of individuals, each one fertilised by the one above and in turn fertilising the one below. Each sea-hare lays several million eggs in a tortuous ribbon wound around the base of seaweeds. (Top plate.)*

Middle: a close relative of the edible winkle, Littorina littoralis *is one of the commonest browsers on* Fucus *in the intertidal region.*

Bottom: a male Gibbula cineraria *releasing a trail of spermatozoa into the water. Substances emitted at the same time provoke the spawning of females in the vicinity.*

Opposite: the opisthobranch Elysia viridis *(15 mm) on* Codium *which is its exclusive food. The green colour which gives it its specific name, is due to algal chloroplasts which are not digested but continue to function in the mollusc's tissues.*

Top: the spawn of Littorina obtusata or a Fucus plant (15 mm).

Bottom: a pair of Lacuna pallidula or red algae. The female is always larger than the male.

Opposite top: limpets on a rocky shore. The different species of limpet are often difficult to distinguish, especially in the Basque region and on the Isle of Wight, where hybridisation occurs.

Opposite bottom: Patina pellucida on a Laminaria frond. For a long time it was thought that there were two species of Patina. The other one was called Patina laevis and is more flattened and lacks the blue lines. They are now known to be the same species; depending where the larvae settle and metamorphose (frond or stipe of the kelp) the adults grow into one or the other form.

Top: the opisthobranch Placida dendritica on a branch of Codium. The giant cells of the Codium, which give it a velvety appearance, can be clearly seen. The digestive gland and reproductive organs of Placida are branched into the processes which cover its back (6 mm).

Bottom: the ormer Haliotis tuberculata progressively closes over the holes in its shell as it grows. At the same time new holes are formed at the edge of the shell. Usually six of these holes remain open and the anus discharges through one of these.

Opposit: Calliostoma zizyphinum laying its eggs. Each yellow dot is an egg, embedded in jelly. In Calliostoma the embryos develop without any swimming planktonic phase. The young ones measure only a quarter of a millimetre and start their life on the sea bed.

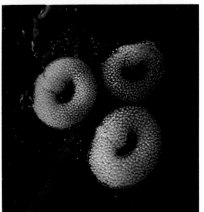

Top: a Zostera *bed at low tide in Santona lagoon on the Spanish Basque coast.*

Middle: these eggs of Lacuna vincta *(8 mm) can be seen in spring. The eggs on the left have just been laid: they are green in colour and more compact. In contrast the eggs at the bottom will soon hatch, as indicated by their whiter colour and more dispersed appearance.*

Bottom: there are several dozen species of the Rissoid family on our coasts; Rissoa membranacea *is one of the species living in* Zostera *beds. It scrapes off the film of diatoms growing on the leaves.*

Opposite: Lacuna vincta *on a* Zostera *leaf. In the prosobranch gastropods the sexes are separate; the more primitive species (Ormers, Topshells, Limpets and Slit-limpets) just release their reproductive products into the sea, but the more advanced species copulate. The male positions himself on the shell of the female and inserts his penis into her gill cavity where the genital opening is located. Winkles or* Lacunas *can often be seen in this position even at low tide.*

In the springtime the Zostera *leaves are covered with the eggs of various molluscs.*

Top: Spawn of Cantharidus striatus.

Middle: spawn of Bittium reticulatum. *The size of the* Zostera *leaf, 5 or 6 mm wide, gives the scale.*

Bottom: the commonest of the two species of Bittium, Bittium reticulatum *prefers to live on the leaves of* Zostera, *but is also found in other habitats. The* Bittiums *belong to the same group as the large ceriths of warmer regions.*

Opposite: in the mini-jungle at the base of the Zostera *plants two* Bittium simplex *move amongst the coralline algae. The two species of* Bittium *occurring in our region have been confused for a long time; they are separated more easily by the colours of the living animals than by the characters of the shell. (See Plate 3.)* Bittium reticulatum *has planktonic larvae while* B. simplex *does not.*

Top: the bivalve Modiolus adriaticu *half-buried in the sediment, is attached by its byssus to the bases of the* Zostera *plants. It filters water in order to feed and respire. There are many other bivalves in the* Zostera *beds but none is characteristic of this habitat.*

Middle: Haminea navicula *lives in the more muddy* Zostera *beds; the shell is not large enough to contain the whole animal (30 mm). The gizzard is armed with three horny plates, but their significance is unknown as the diet of the animal is a mystery. The gelatinous spawn (35 mm) is deposited on* Zostera *leaves in late spring and in summer.*

Bottom: these little transparent urns (6 mm), usually deposited in lines of a dozen, contain the eggs of the netted dog-whelk, Nassarius reticulatus. *Swimming larvae hatch out of them and spend more than a month in the plankton before metamorphosing into little crawling whelks. It is no good searching for this dog-whelk alongside its eggs, as it lives buried in the sand or mud, with only its sensory siphon sticking out, like a periscope. The siphon detects any odours, and when a dead body is located the dog-whelks come out of the sand and head for the body at top speed.*

Opposite: a dog-whelk cleaning out a dead crab with its proboscis.

fauna of the rocks

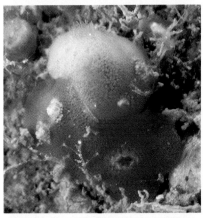

Preceding page: the nudibranch Archidoris tuberculata *is a frequent inhabitant of the boulder fields, especially in March or April, when it is spawning. Illustrated here (top) is an animal laying its scalloped ribbon of hundreds of thousands of eggs on the rock.*

Middle: nudibranchs are all hermaphrodites, the very complex genital apparatus opening on the right-hand side of the body, behind the head. Here are two Rostanga rubra *(12 mm) mating head to tail.*

Bottom: the spawn (35 mm) of Hypselodoris valenciennesi. *It is nearly possible to recognise the spawn of each species of mollusc, but it can always be recognised to generic level.*

Opposite: Hypselodoris valenciennesi *(35 mm) from the Basque coast. The plume of gills surrounding the anus is particularly obvious. The* Hypselodoris *like the* Chromodoris *on the following page belongs to a tropical family which reaches its northern limits on our Atlantic coast.* H. valenciennesi *can be found in summer as far north as the Plateau of Rochebonne near the Ile d'Yeu.*

Top: this Onchidoris *has just laid its spiral spawn on the aquarium glass. It is easy to see the brown digestive gland through the transparent animal.*

Upper middle: Chromodoris purpurea *is one of the most colourful nudibranchs of our region; it is only found on the Basque coast.*

Lower middle: the keyhole limpet Diodora apertura *feeds on sponges by scraping pieces off with its radula. Sponges are protected by spicules of silica, which form a skeleton of glass wool, but this does not trouble the keyhole limpet. The indigestible parts are simply surrounded by mucus and ejected through the anus.*

Bottom: Triforis perversa *is a close relative of* Bittium *but has a sinistral shell. It is found on sponges with* Cerithiopsis *species which are dextral.*

Opposite: the Aeolid Coryphella pedata *eating a polyp of the hydroid* Eudendrium.

Top: The nudibranch Aeolidia papillosa *is the largest Aeolid in our region; it is usually found in spring when it is spawning. An* Aeolidia *is approaching a sea-anemone* Cereus pedunculatus. *It withdraws its fragile sensory tentacles to the maximum amount and starts to bite the column of the anemone. The* Cereus *reacts violently throwing out over the nudibranch white filaments packed with poison cells. The* Aeolidia *secretes large amounts of mucus to protect itself and is generally victorious. The anemone will be eaten in one night.*

Upper middle: The dorid Doriopsilla areolata *has neither radula nor jaws and for a long time people wondered how it ever ate. In fact it evaginates a part of its digestive system over a sponge, secretes enzymes which digest the sponge to make a broth, and then swallows the lot!*

Lower middle: The Pleurobranchacean Berthella plumula *(30 mm) protects itself from its enemies by acid glands in its naked skin.*

Bottom: The nudibranch Jorunna tomentosa *on the sponge* Adocia simulans. *The molluscs which attack sponges do not all eat the same species. Each species has several very strict preferences. This reduction of competition results in maximum exploitation of the food resources of the habitat.*

Opposite: The ovulid Simnia patula *amongst Dead-men's fingers. It is the only representative in our region of a tropical family; all the species feed on Gorgonians or Alcyonarians (soft corals) and are often well camouflaged on their food.*

Top: in the middle of the cerata of Spurilla neapolitana *(30 mm) the violet egg-sacs of the copepod parasite* Splanchnotrophus dellechiajei *can be seen. This little crustacean lives inside the nudibranch and only its egg-sacs are extruded to the outside. On hatching the swimming larvae will contaminate new* Spurilla. Spurilla *with parasites do not die but are unable to reproduce and the parasites therefore control the populations of* Spurilla *and the populations of sea-anemones on which the nudibranch feeds.*

Middle: The Aeolid Facelina annuli-cornis *(25 mm).*

Bottom: Trinchesia aurantia *(12 mm) amongst a bouquet of* Tubularia *which it is eating.*

Opposite: Facelina coronata *(18 mm) crawling amongst hydroids. Sometimes individuals are found which have completely blue cerata. In all Aeolids the digestive gland is branched into all the numerous cerata covering the back. At the tip of each ceratum is a small sac in which the stinging cells from the hydroids or sea-anemones are stored. Thus not only is the Aeolid completely unharmed by eating the hydroid, but the stinging cells are stored for use when needed against any predators which would attack the Aeolid.*

Top: the bivalve Galeomma turtoni *lives with its valves wide open, more or less stuck beneath the rocks. Like the Gastropods it is able to crawl on its foot. Very little is known about its biology.*

Top middle: Trinchesia caerulea *on a branch of the hydroid* Sertularella.

Bottom middle: the Aeolid Eubranchus pallidus *(12 mm).*

Bottom: Berghia verrucicornis *(15 mm). Some zoologists interpret the bright colours of nudibranchs as warning colouration. Thus the fish which has had one experience of an inedible nudibranch learns to associate the character "not nice to eat" with the character "bright colour". At the next encounter with a colourful nudibranch the fish knows it is inedible and does not try to eat it. This is of advantage to the mollusc as it may be injured or killed by the attention of the fish.*

Opposite: Doto koenneckeri, *one of the group* Doto coronata *(10 mm) amongst hydroids; its spawn is attached alongside it.*

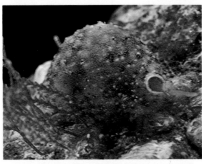

Top: three Favorinus branchialis *(12 mm) eating the eggs of the doric* Goniodoris nodosa *(top, middle) which itself feeds on the red ascidian* Dendrodoa *which coats rocky overhangs in the Channel. Its spawn consists of a large white noodle stuck out of the ascidian, containing thousands of eggs coated in a jelly. The* Favorinus *have eaten most of the eggs of* Goniodoris, *only the jelly and a few scattered eggs remain, while the white eggs are being digested in the cerata of the Aeolid.* Favorinus *feeds only on the eggs of other nudibranchs.*

Botton middle: do not rely on appearances! Lamellaria *is not a nudibranch but a prosobranch whose shell is internal, totally covered by the mantle. It feeds on compound ascidians on which its cryptic colouration makes it difficult to see.*

Bottom: the bivalve Musculus marmoratus *usually lives in the cellulose tunic of large ascidians. Often the tunic is encrusted with bryozoans, algae or sponges (as is the case here) and the bivalve is only in contact with the outside world through a straight chimney.*

Opposite: Trivia *is able to cover its shell completely with its mantle lobes, which secrete a varnish. It is this behaviour that gives the tropical cowries their bright glossy shells.*

Top: a group of Limacia clavigera *(12 mm) on seaweed covered with the bryozoan* Electra pilosa *which they eat.*

Middle: the dorid Polycera quadrilineata *also feeds on bryozoans. Some individuals are spotted with black.*

Bottom: Polycera dubia *is very difficult to see because of its camouflage colouration.*

Opposite: Antiopella cristata *(30 mm) is found on the large erect bryozoan* Bugula tubinata *which is its sole food.*

Top left: Chlamys varia *attached under a rock by its byssus.*

Top right: the thick-lipped dog-whelk, Nassarius reticulatus.

Middle: a saddle-oyster, Anomia ephippium. *The upper valve is open and the orange genital mass can be seen inside. Bivalves do not mate. Eggs and spermatozoa are discharged liberally into the water where fertilisation takes place.*

Bottom: byssus of a saddle-oyster on the rock, after the death of the animal.

Opposite, top: the sting winkle, Ocenebra erinacea. *Like the Murexes of the tropics the* Ocenebra *of our regions feed by boring holes in bivalve shells using their radulae and an acid. We have three species of* Ocenebra *on our coasts one of which,* O. edwardsi *is restricted to the south. A closely related species* Urosalpinx cinerea *was accidentally introduced around 1920 with American oysters and is a pest for the oyster farmers. At the moment it is restricted to the southeast of England.*

Bottom: in February the Ocenebra *assemble under the heaviest boulders to lay their eggs. This is a large aggregation at the low tide mark.*

Top: a holothurian of the genus Cucumaria *beneath a block in the infra littoral zone. It is parasitised by two* Balcis crosseana *(upper middle, 4 mm) which have no radula. These gastro pods feed by piercing the skin of the holothurian with their proboscis. There are about 15 species of Eulimids in our region, all are very difficult to identify. Very little is known about their biology but it is certain that they are all parasitic on Echinoderms.*

Lower middle: the bivalve Irus irus *lives in crevices in rocks.*

The polyplacophorans Lepidochitona ci nereus *(bottom 15 mm) and* Acantho chitona discrepans *(opposite 35 mm) live beneath rocks in the intertidal region where they scrape off algae with their radulae. The radula is very hard and mineralised so that it can stand up to this abuse.*

fauna of the estuaries

Preceding page: the gastropod Hydrobia ulvae *is certainly one of the commonest if not the commonest animal of Atlantic shores. Tens of millions live in each estuary and in some places there are so many that the sand is entirely made up of their dead shells. (Bottom.) They feed on organic material extracted from the mud which they ingest.*

Top: the bivalve Abra alba *forms vast populations on the mudflats, buried under several millimetres of sediment. All the members of the genus* Abra *live in muddy habitats.*

Upper middle: the plumonate gastropod Phytia myosotis *lives under drift wood deposited high on the saltmarsh. The salt water only reaches it on a few occasions in the year.*

Lower middle: as well as living in large numbers in crevices in the splash zone Lasaea rubra *is also found under scarcely humid stones on the saltmarsh. In order to survive in these harsh environments* Lasaea *must incubate its young in its branchial cavity. At birth they have never seen the open sea and are already capable of providing for all their needs.*

Opposite: Siphons of a cockle emerging from muddy sand.

Previous page: the siphons of a razor-shell emerging from the sand.

Top left: siphons of the carpet-shell, Tapes decussatus.

Upper middle: siphons of Tapes aureus.

Lower middle: siphons of Cardium crassum.

Bottom: siphons of Gari depressa.

The siphons of bivalves are just as reliable a character for identification as their shells and their shell hinges.

Top right: a venus shell Venus verrucosa *half buried.*

Below: Cardium crassum; *a cockle of our shores.*

Opposite top: Tapes aureus, *half buried in sand. The colour pattern of this shell is very variable but whether this variation is inherited is not known at the present time. In the last century some shell collectors used to amuse themselves by giving names to all these individual varieties!*

Below: Venus fasciata.

Left: different stages in the burrowing of the trough-shell Spisula solida. *In this operation the contractile foot clearly plays an important part but the respiratory cavity and siphons also assist. The foot of sedentary species (Chlamys, oysters) is very much reduced; on the contrary that of* Thyasira *can reach out 18 times the diameter of the shell.*

Top: the large necklace-shell, Natica catena *boring into a bivalve which it is holding tightly in its foot. The bivalve has no chance of escaping!*

Below: the little necklace-shell, Natica alderi *beside its spawn.*

Opposite top: the spawn of Natica catena.

Bottom: the spawn of Natica alderi.

Top: two species characteristic of exposed sandy beaches, Mactra corallina and Donax vittatus.

Lower middle: as in Haminea the shell of Philine cannot contain the animal. In Philine aperta, the largest of the genus (30 mm) the shell is internal and does not protect the animal at all. The digestive system contains calcareous plates which crush the small bivalves and foraminiferans on which Philine feeds. These yellowish plates can be seen inside the semi-transparent animal.

Bottom: two wentletraps, Clathrus clathrus. Little is known about the diet of the wentletraps of our regions. It is known that some tropical and mediterranean species pierce the skin of sea-anemones and suck out their body fluids. It is likely that our species feed in this way but it has never been observed.

Opposite: the edible winkle, Littorina littorea. This winkle does not deposit its eggs in a gelatinous mass like the others we have seen. The eggs are released into the sea in little capsules containing 2, 3 or 4 eggs and measuring only 1 mm. It is no good searching for the eggs of this winkle!

Top: a pair of chinaman's-hat shell Calyptraea chinensis in an empty shell the smaller individual being the male These shells are rather like limpets but they feed in a completely different manner, by filtering microscopic alga out of the plankton while the limpet browse on algae on rock surfaces.

Upper middle: a whelk, Buccinum undatum in a Zostera bed. The whelk has been the object of a small fishery in the Channel for a long time, where it is called Ran, Bulot, Calicoco or Escargo de Mer. Very abundant in the west of the Province it gave rise to a specialist fisherman at the turn of the century each fisherman could collect as many as 200 on each tide.

Lower middle: close up of the head, the very small eye can be seen, it plays no part in searching for food but can only distinguish light and shade.

Bottom: the hatching of young whelks. When it is laid, each capsule contains hundreds of eggs, but only about twenty develop and eat the others which are called nutritive eggs. When the supply of nutritive eggs is exhausted the stronger embryos eat the weaker ones. After two months only a dozen young whelks remain to hatch.

Opposite: Gibbula magus crawling over gravel.

Top: Caecum imperforatum, *a very common animal in well sorted coarse sand. The sand grain gives the scale; on it is a little white spot, this is an egg of* Caecum! *When it hatches the shell is coiled normally but when it grows it becomes comma-shaped and then the coiled end falls off.*

Upper middle: Tornus subcarinatus *which lives under rocks buried in the sand (2 mm).*

Lower middle: the small interstitial opisthobranch Retusa truncatula *(3 mm) feeds on very small bivalves and foraminiferans which it finds in the sand.*

Bottom: the bivalve Pseudopythina setosa *reaches the northern limits of its distribution on the coasts of Finistère. Nothing is known about its biology.*

Opposite: the Rissoid Alvania lactea *(. mm) lives beneath rocks buried in the sand.*

shellfish farming

Previous page: several hectares of posts in the Bay of Aiguillon, to the north of La Rochelle. This bay in the mouth of the Sèvre is the oldest and most important region of mussel-farming in France. Some figures will give an idea: 10,000 tons of mussels per year, 650 square kilometres of a million wooden posts.

Top: two native oysters in the wild. In the natural situation the oysters are never detached, and they spend all their life stuck to the spot where they settled, which is in this case a boulder.

Upper middle: a chain of slipper-limpets, Crepidula fornicata *in a badly-maintained oyster bed. When it is young the slipper-limpet is male, and attaches itself to the top of a chain. As it grows it changes sex and becomes a female. The little individuals are male and fertilise the older animals at the base of the chain.*

Lower middle: this dog-whelk Nucella lapillus *seen at low tide, is boring into a mussel. Dog-whelks also attack other prey, especially barnacles despite their protection of thick calcareous walls.*

Bottom: the eggs of the dog-whelk.

Opposite: when the mussel opens its valves to filter water, Odostomia scalaris *sticks in its proboscis and sucks up the haemolymph of the bivalve. When resting it hides in the byssus of the mussel where it also lays its eggs.*

Following page: the Tremblade, haven of the Japanese oyster.

fauna of the open sea

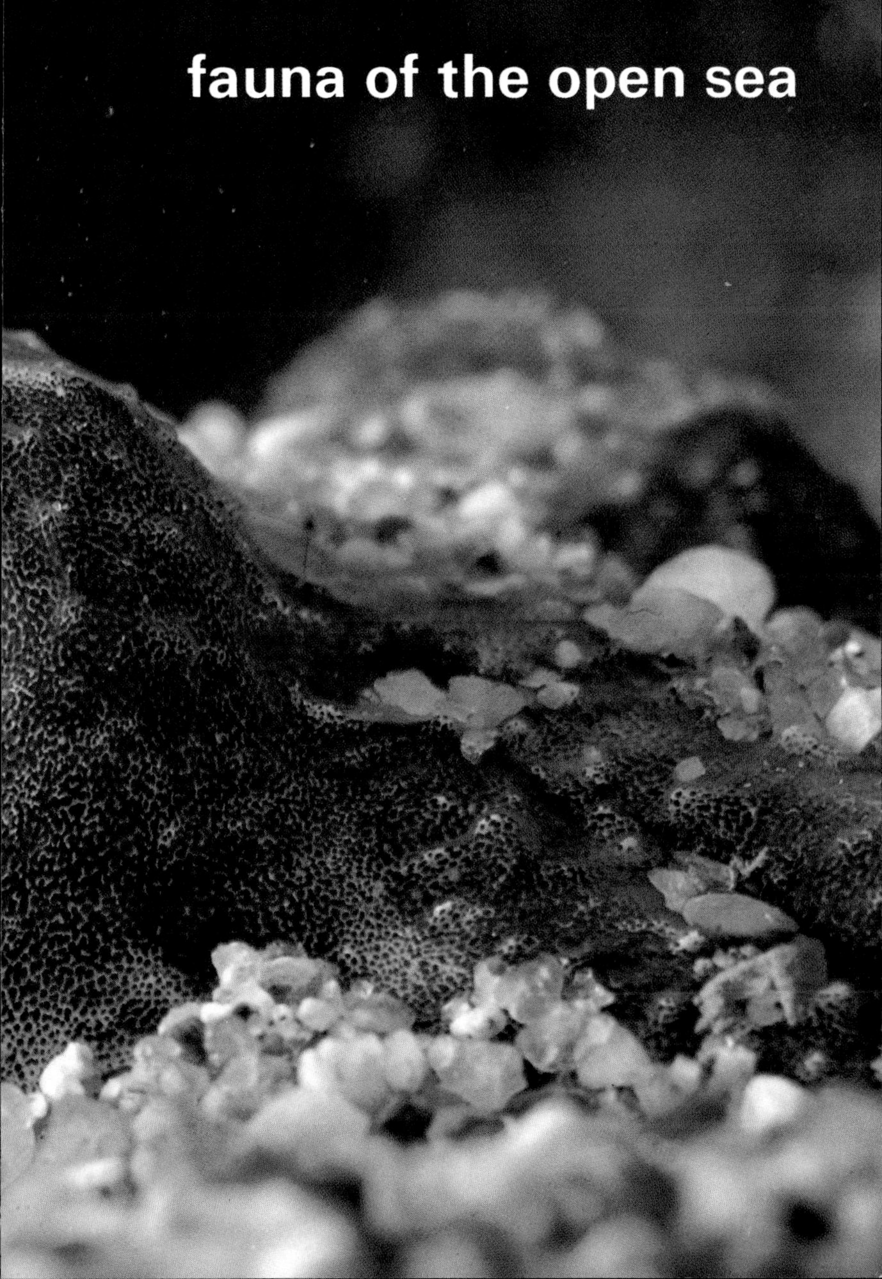

Previous page: a cuttlefish camouflaged in the sand.

Top: hunting with a harpoon Philbertia purpurea *feeds on small worms. They are also found in the* Laminaria *zone.* Philbertia *is the most highly evolved genus of prosobranchs on our coasts.*

Middle: Cantharidus exasperatus, *a small topshell occurring on maerl.*

Bottom: the maerl chiton, Callochiton laevis *laying its eggs (12 mm). In the polyplacophorans, as in the bivalves, there is no mating; males and females release their gametes freely into the water, where fertilisation occurs.*

Oppnsite: Tricolia pullus. *Unlike other prosobranchs the operculum of* Tricolia *is not just a thin horny plate, it is a thick calcareous button, like that of the large exotic Turbos.*

Top: sea raisins. The cuttlefish Sepia officinalis *migrate into the* Zostera *beds to lay their large black eggs, which are attached in groups to the plants.*

Middle: the eggs of the common squid Loligo vulgaris *attached to the roof of an underwater cave.*

Bottom: the pallial eye of a great scallop. The eyes of scallops do not form a true image, but merely inform the animal of changes in illumination.

Opposite: an inhabitant of the soft, muddy bottoms of the open sea, Aporrhais pespelecani *feeds on organic detritus on the bottom.*

Top: another hunter with a harpoon,
Philbertia linearis, *lives on gravel*
bottoms in the infra-littoral zone.

Middle: Balcis alba *is the largest Eulima*
of our region. Like B. crosseana *it is*
also parasitic on the holothurian
Pseudocucumis mixta, *which lives in*
offshore coarse sands.

Bottom: the tiny bivalve Montacuta
substriata *is attached by a byssus thread*
to a spine of the burrowing sea-urchin
Spatangus. *There are about six species*
of Montacuta *in our region, living*
commensally with various echinoderms.

Opposite: the mantle edge of Lima hians
carries flamboyant tentacles. When
attacked by a predator these tentacles
can break off and discharge an acid
secretion. Lima *can swim but*
normally lives in a nest of shell debris
stuck together with mucus.

Following page: a young squid (3 mm) a
few minutes old. The chromatophores,
huge in comparison with its size, can
expand or contract in a fraction of a
second.

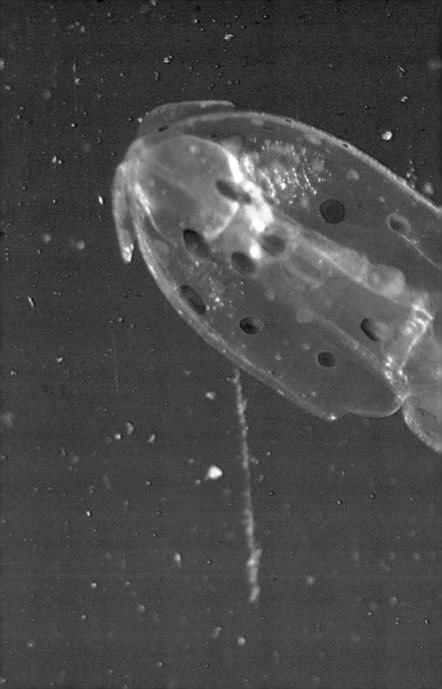

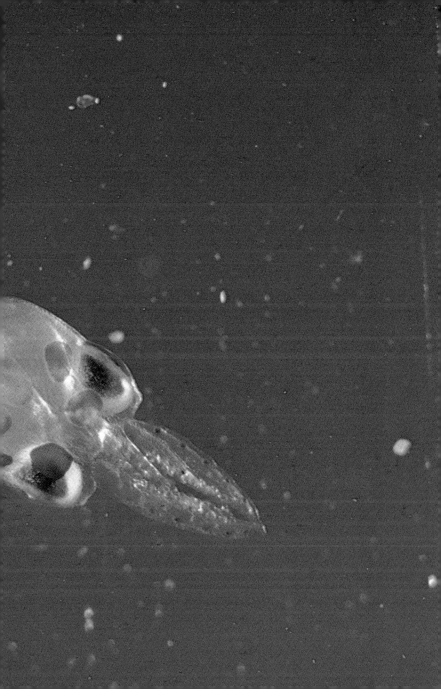

plate 1
× 0.9

1. **Haliotis tuberculata** *(Haliotidae) - Ormer - rocky shores in the infra-littoral.*

2. **Patella vulgata** *(Patellidae) Limpet - bare rocks of the middle shore.*

3. **Patella aspera** *(Patellidae) Limpet - bare rocks of the middle shore.*

4. **Patina pellucida** *(Patellidae) Blue-rayed Limpet - on* **Laminaria** *; on the left the form* **Laevis.**

5. **Patella intermedia** *(Patellidae) Limpet - bare rocks of the middle shore.*

6. **Patella lusitanica** *(Patellidae) Limpet - rocks of the middle shore - only on the Basque coast.*

7. **Diodora apertura** *(Fissurellidae) Keyhole Limpet - rocky shores in the infra-littoral.*

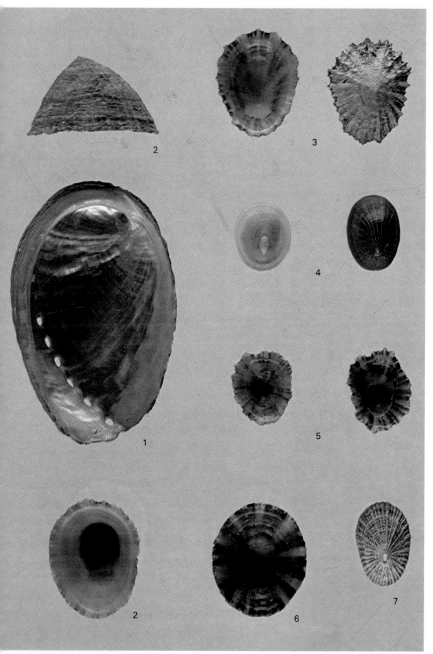

plate 2
× 0.9

1. **Gibbula pennanti** *(Trochidae) Topshell - weeds and boulders of the infra-littoral.*

2. **Gibbula umbilicalis** *(Trochidae) Topshell - weeds and rocks.*

3. **Gibbula cineraria** *(Trochidae) Gray topshell - weeds and rocks of the infra-littoral. 3a: the sub-species* **cineraria** *found on all our coasts except the Basque coast where it is replaced by the sub-species* **strigosa** *(3b).*

4. **Calliostoma zizyphinum** *(Trochidae) Painted topshell - weeds and rocks from the infra-littoral to 80 m.*

5. **Calliostoma granulatum** *(Trochidae) Topshell - from 20 m down.*

6. **Monodonta lineata** *(Trochidae) Bare rocks of the supra- and mid-littoral.*

7. **Gibbula magus** *(Trochidae) Topshell - gravelly bottoms in the infra-littoral.*

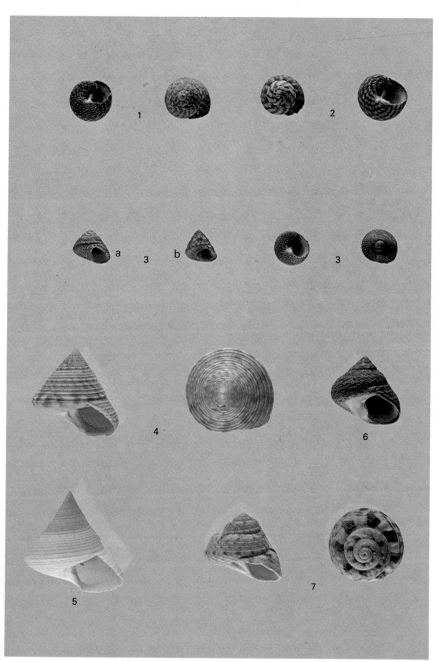

plate 3
× 1.2

1. **O c e n e b r a   c o r a l l i n a** *(Muricidae) - Rocky shores in the infra-littoral - a southern species.*

2. **O c e n e b r a   e d w a r d s i** *(Muricidae) - Rocky shores in the infra-littoral, only on the Basque coast.*

3. **Nassarius incrassatus** *(Nassariidae) - Rocky shores in the infra-littoral.*

4. **Philbertia purpurea** *(Turridae) - boulders and gravels of the infra-littoral.*

5. **Balcis alba** *(Eulimidae) sandy bottoms at about 20 m.*

6. **Bittium simplex** *(Cerithiidae)* **Zostera** *beds - infra-littoral - a southern species.*

7. **Triforis adversa** *(Triforidae) boulders of the infra-littoral.*

8. **Bittium reticulatum** *(Cerithiidae) beds of* **Zostera** *and seaweeds of the mid- and infra-littoral.*

9. **Lacuna vincta** *(Lacunidae)* **Zostera** *beds and seaweeds of the infra-littoral.*

10. **Lacuna pallidula** *(Lacunidae) Red algae in the infra-littoral.*

11. **Trivia arctica** *(Eratoidae) boulders in the infra-littoral.*

12. **Trivia monacha** *(Eratoidae) Cowrie - boulders in the infra-littoral.*

13. *A young* **Trivia** *shell.*

14. **Littorina littoralis** *(Littorinidae). Flat winkle - seaweeds in the mid-littoral.*

15. **Littorina littorea** *(Littorinidae) Edible winkle - pebbles in the mid-littoral.*

16. **Littorina saxatilis** *(Littorinidae) Rough winkle - bare rocks of the upper shore.*

17. **Natica alderi** *(Naticidae) Necklace-shell - infra-littoral sands.*

18. **Crepidula fornicata** *(Calyptraeidae) Slipper limpet - oyster beds, shingle on the middle and lower shore.*

19. **Calyptraea chinensis** *(Calyptraeidae) Chinaman's hat - gravels and empty shells in the infra-littoral.*

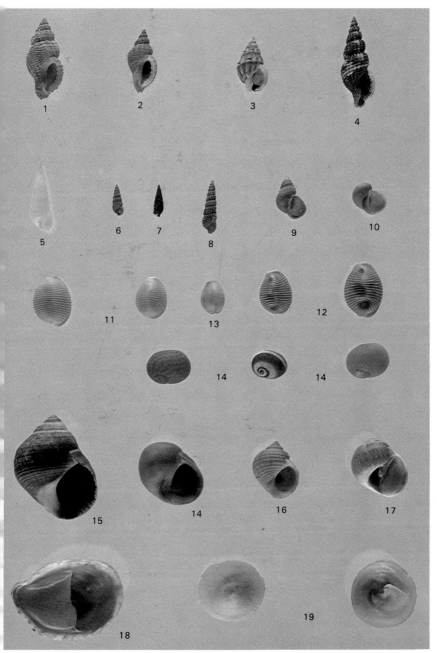

plate 4
× 0.75

1. **Nucella lapillus** *(Muricidae) Dogwhelk - rocky shores, mid-littoral - on the left the form* **imbricata.**

2. **Nassarius reticulatus** *(Nassariidae) - netted dog-whelk - sand and gravel of the middle and lower shore.*

3. **Natica catena** *(Naticidae) Necklace-shell - infra-littoral sands.*

4. **Ocenebra erinacea** *(Muricidae) sting winkle - infra-littoral boulders.*

5. **Acteon tornatilis** *(Actaeonidae) infra-littoral sands.*

6. **Haminea hydatis** *(Atyidae) Coarse sands and* **Zostera** *beds - infra-littoral.*

7 . **B u c c i n u m u n d a t u m** *(Buccinidae) Whelk - infra-littoral gravel and boulders - below - the form* **acuminatum** *common on the shore of Cotentin.*

8. **Dentalium vulgare** *(Dentalidae) Tusk-shell - infra-littoral sands.*

9. **Turritella communis** *(Turritellidae) Auger-shell - infra-littoral sands.*

10. **Clathrus clathrus** *(Epitoniidae) Wentletrap - infra-littoral sands.*

11. **Opalia crenata** *(Epitoniidae) Wentletrap - infra-littoral gravels - only on the Basque coast.*

12. **Scaphander lignarius** *(Scaphandridae) sand and gravel - 10 to 300 metres.*

13. **Aporrhais pespelecani** *(Aporrhaidae) Pelicans foot - mud and sandy mud - infra-littoral to 300 m - on the right form* **bilobatus** *from the coasts of Charente-Maritime.*

plate 5
× 5
small molluscs

1. **Rissoa parva** *(Rissoidae) Weeds of the middle and lower shore.*
2. **Cingula semicostata** *(Rissoidae) Weeds and infra-littoral gravels.*
3. **Balcis crosseana** *(Eulimidae) infra-littoral boulders.*
4. **Odostomia scalaris** *(Pyramidellidae) in mussel beds.*
5. **Assiminea littorina** *(Assimineidae) Estuarine saltmarsh - southern species - northern limit, the Bay of St. Malo.*
6. **Lasaea rubra** *(Erycinidae) Crevices in the middle and upper shore - also estuarine saltmarshes.*
7. **Astarte triangularis** *(Astartidae) Coarse infra-littoral sands.*
8. **Caecum imperforatum** *(Caecidae) Coarse infra-littoral sands.*
9. **Alvania semistriata** *(Rissoidae) Infra-littoral weeds and gravel.*
10. **Cingula cingillus** *(Rissoidae) Middle shore boulders and crevices.*
11. **Hydrobia ulvae** *(Hydrobiidae) Estuarine mudflats.*
12. **Assiminea grayana** *(Assimineidae) Estuarine saltmarsh - only in the eastern English Channel.*
13. **Alvania lactea** *(Rissoidae) Sandy boulders - infra-littoral.*
14. **Littorina neritoides** *(Littorinidae) Bare rocks, crevices and small algae - supra-littoral.*
15. **Pseudomelampus exiguus** *(Ellobiidae) Estuarine saltmarsh, only on the Basque coast.*
16. **Phytia myosotis** *(Ellobiidae) - Estuarine saltmarsh.*
17. **Vasconiella jeffreysi** *(Erycinidae) Habitat unknown - (never seen alive!) - only on the Basque coast.*
18. **Rissoa membranacea** *(Rissoidae)* **Zostera** *beds - infra-littoral.*

plate 6
× 1.3

1. **Cantharidus exasperatus** *(Trochidae) Red algae: maerl - infra-littoral.*

2. **Cantharidus montagui** *(Trochidae) Coarse sand: gravel - 5 to 20 metres.*

3. **Gibbula tumida** *(Trochidae) Offshore gravel 10 to 100 m.*

4. **Tricolia pullus** *(Turbinidae) Pheasant-shell - weeds and maerl, infra-littoral.*

5. **Emarginula reticulata** *(Fissurellidae) Slit limpet - boulders - infra-littoral to 80 metres.*

6. **Patelloidea virginea** *(Acmaeidae) boulders, stones and empty shells - infra-littoral.*

7. **Loripes lucinalis** *(Lucinidae) hatchet-shell - infra-littoral sand and gravel.*

8. **Thyasira flexuosa** *(Thyasiridae) infra-littoral mud of estuaries.*

9. **Divaricella divaricata** *(Lucinidae) Infra-littoral sand - only as far north as Scilly Is.*

10. **Musculus marmoratus** *(Mytilidae) in the tunic of ascidians, sometimes free.*

11. **Arca lactea** *(Arcidae) Infra-littoral boulders.*

12. **Nucula nucleus** *(Nuculidae) coarse sand - infra-littoral to 100 m.*

13. **Pseudopythina setosa** *(Erycinidae) Under rocks on sand - infra-littoral, northern limit of distribution at Brest.*

14. **Tellina tenuis** *(Tellinidae) fine sand - mid- and infra-littoral.*

15. **Abra alba** *(Scrobicularidae) Estuarine mudflats.*

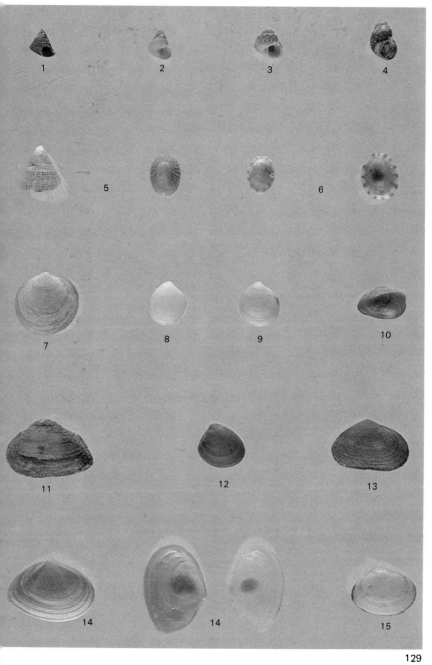

plate 7
× 0.8

1. **Glycymeris glycymeris** *(Glycymeridae) Dog cockle infra-littoral coarse sand.*
2. **Tellina squalida** *(Tellinidae) Infra-littoral coarse sand.*
3. **Lucinoma borealis** *(Lucinidae) Hatchet-shell. Infra-littoral sand.*
4. **Macoma balthica** *(Tellinidae) Estuarine mudflats.*
5. **Diplodonta rotundata** *(Diplodontidae) Infra-littoral sand and gravel.*
6. **Anomia ephippium** *(Anomiidae) Saddle-oyster - infra-littoral boulders.*
7. **Lima hians** *(Limidae) Offshore mixed mud and shell to 80 m.*
8. **Modiolus barbatus** *(Mytilidae) Infra-littoral crevices and boulders.*
9. **Modiolus adriaticus** *(Mytilidae)* **Zostera** *beds, infra-littoral gravels.*
10. **Tellina crassa** *(Tellinidae) Infra-littoral sands.*
11. **Chlamys distorta** *(Pectinidae) Infra-littoral boulders.*
12. **Gastrana fragilis** *(Tellinidae) No longer to be found alive in our region, this is a relic of colder times, the empty shells are not uncommon.*

131

plate 8
× 0.6

1. **Cardium crassum** *(Cardiidae)* - coarse sand, infra-littoral zone.
2. **Cardium aculeatum** *(Cardiidae)* - infra-littoral sand and coarse sand.
3. **Cardium paucicostatum** *(Cardiidae)* - infra-littoral sand - northern limit of distribution the Bay of Quiberon, but present in the Bay of Mont St. Michel.
4. **Dosinia exoleta** *(Veneridae)* - infra-littoral sand and gravel.
5. **Dosinia lupinus** *(Veneridae)* - infra-littoral mud and sand.
6. **Venus ovata** *(Veneridae)* - infra-littoral sand and gravel.
7. **Venus fasciata** *(Veneridae)* - infra-littoral sand.
8. **Pandora albida** *(Pandoridae)* - infra-littoral sand.
9. **Tapes rhomboides** *(Veneridae)* - infra-littoral sand.
10. **Gari depressa** *(Garidae)* - infra-littoral sand.
11. **Irus irus** *(Veneridae)* - in crevices in infra-littoral boulders.
12. **Mactra glauca** *(Mactridae)* - trough-shell - infra-littoral sand.
13. **Scrobicularia plana** *(Scrobiculariidae)* - estuarine mudflats.
14. **Mactra corallina** *(Mactridae)* - fine infra-littoral sand.

plate 9
× 0.7
edible bivalves

1. **Donax variegatus** *(Donacidae)* - *infra-littoral sands.*

2. **Donax truculus** *(Donacidae) - fine sand on surf beaches. Northern limit of distribution is Brest.*

3. **Donax vittatus** *(Donacidae) - infra-littoral fine sand on exposed beaches.*

4. **Tapes aureus** *(Veneridae) - sand of the mid- and infra-littoral.*

5. **Tapes pullastra** *(Veneridae) - mid- and infra-littoral sand.*

6. **Venus striatula** *(Veneridae) - mid- and infra-littoral sand.*

7. **Spisula solida** *(Mactridae) - trough-shell - infra-littoral sand.*

8. **Tapes decussatus** *(Veneridae) - carpet-shell - infra-littoral sand and gravel.*

9. **Cardium edule** *(Cardiidae) - cockle - sand and muddy sand, middle shore.*

10. **Venus verrucosa** *(Veneridae) - Venus clam - infra-littoral sand.*

11. **Cardium tuberculatum** *(Cardiidae) - infra-littoral sand.*

12. **Mytilus edulis** *(Mytilidae) - mussel - on rocks and cultivated - middle shore.*

13. **Mytilus galloprovincialis** *(Mytilidae) - mid-littoral on rocks.*

plate 10
× 0.5
edible bivalves

1. **Chlamys opercularis** *(Pectinidae)* - *Queen Scallop* - *infra-littoral mud and sand.*

2. **Chlamys varia** *(Pectinidae)* - *infra-littoral boulders.*

3. **Pecten maximus** *(Pectinidae)* - *Great Scallop. Sand and gravel bottoms from the infra-littoral to 80 m.*

4. **Callista chione** *(Veneridae)* - *infra-littoral sand.*

5. **Mercenaria mercenaria** *(Veneridae)* - *Quahog or clam. Infra-littoral mud in estuaries. Introduced from the American Atlantic coast.*

6. **Ensis siliqua** *(Solenidae)* - *razor-shell - infra-littoral sand.*

7. **Ensis ensis** *(Solenidae)* - *razor-shell - fine infra-littoral sand.*

8. **Mya arenaria** *(Myidae)* - *Gaper - estuarine mud - introduced from North America in the 17th century.*

9. **Lutraria lutraria** *(Lutrariidae)* - *otter shell - infra-littoral sand and coarse sand.*

137

plate 11
× 0.9
drillers and borers

1. **Hiatella arctica** *(Hiatellidae)* - in crevices and in the empty holes of other borers - infra-littoral.

2. **Gastrochaena dubia** *(Gastrochaenidae)* - in calcareous algae and sedimentary rocks - infra-littoral.

3. **Lithophaga aristata** *(Mytilidae)* - in calcareous algae, barnacle encrustations, or the shells of large gastropods. Mid- and infra-littoral zones. Only on the Basque coast.

4. **Zirfaea crispata** *(Pholadidae)* - in sedimentary infra-littoral rocks.

5. **Petricola lithophaga** *(Petricolidae)* - in sedimentary rocks middle and lower shore. Northern limit of distribution the Loire.

6. **Barnea candida** *(Pholadidae)* - in chalk, mudstones and sometimes wood, infra-littoral.

7. **Pholas dactylus** *(Pholadidae)* - piddock - sedimentary rocks and mustones - infra-littoral.

8. Result of action of the boring sponge **Cliona celata** on a venus-shell.

9. Trough-shells bored by necklace-shells.

139

index of scientific names

A.

Abra alba : 88, 128
Acanthochitona
   discrepans : 85
Acteon tornatilis : 124
Aegires punctilucens : 14
Aeolidia papillosa : 21, 72, 73
Alderia : 29
Alexia bidentata : 28
Alvania : 35, 101, 126.
Alvania lactea : 101, 126.
Alvania semistriata : 126
Anomia
   ephippium : 82, 130
Antiopella cristata : 20, 81
Aplacophores : 7
Aplysia : 12, 52, 54
Aporrhais
   pespelicani : 44, 113, 128
Arca lactea : 128
Archidoris
   tuberculata : 18, 66, 68
Armina : 44
Assiminea eliae : 28
Assiminea grayana : 28, 126
Assiminea littorina : 126
Assiminea ostiorum : 28
Astarte triangularis : 126

B.

Balcis alba : 114, 122
Balcis
   crosseana : 24, 84, 126.
Barnea candida : 138
Berghia : 21, 76
Berthella : 19, 72
Bittium
   reticulatum : 14, 62, 122

Bittium
   simplex : 14, 63, 122
Bivalve : 6, 7
Buccinum
   undatum : 34, 98, 124

C.

Caecum : 34, 100
Caecum imperforatum : 126
Calliostoma
   granulatum : 120
Calliostoma
   zizyphinum : 13, 59, 120
Callista chione : 136
Callochiton laevis : 44, 110
Calyptraea
   sinensis : 98, 122
Cantharidus : 44, 110
Cantharidus
   exasperatus : 128
Cantharidus montagui : 128
Cantharidus striatus : 14, 62
Cardium aculeatum : 132
Cardium crassum :
   32, 92, 132
Cardium edule : 32, 134
Cardium lamarcki : 28
Cardium
   paucicostatum : 132.
Cardium
   tuberculatum : 32, 134
Carpet-shell : 30, 92, 134
Chiton : 6, 7
Chlamys distorta : 22, 130
Chlamys opercularis : 136
Chlamys varia : 22, 82, 136
Chromodoris
   purpurea : 19, 70
Cingula cingillus : 126
Cingula semicostata : 126
Clam : 39, 136
Clathrus
   clathrus : 33, 96, 124
Cockle : 32, 88, 92, 93, 134

BIBLIOGRAPHY

British Prosobranch Molluscs
V. Fretter and A. Graham, 1962
Royal Society, London.

British Shells
N. F. McMillan, 1968
Frederick Warne, London.

Ocean Life in Colour
Norman and Olga Marshall, 1971
Blandford Press, Poole.

Encyclopaedia of Shells
Edited by S. Peter Dance, 1974
Blandford Press, Poole.

British Bivalve Seashells
N. Tebbe, 1966
British Museum (Natural History), London.

Seashore Life in Colour
Gwynne Vevers, 1969
Blandford Press, Poole.

British Opisthobranch Molluscs
T. Thompson & G. Brown, 1976
Academic Press, London.

Seashells of the World
Gert Lindner, 1977
Blandford Press, Poole.

Printed in Japan
1979